THE DEAN: ON DUTY

An Experience in Education

Glenn Swanson

CONTENTS

With sincere thanks to all the people who have helped me through this effort by providing insight, critique, advice, and support throughout the process; with appreciation for the school for providing me the opportunity in a sabbatical and the means to accomplish the writing; with recognition to all the students I have known who have struggled through the journey called adolescence; with dedication to Persis and Calvin, who live always in the forefront of my work; and for Estey, without whose encouragement and support this work would never have happened.

APOLOGIA

I live on campus at a boarding/day school of teenagers in grades 9-12, with an additional day population in the 7th and 8th grades that has a separate administrator. Even though only a small portion of the American population has contact with or knowledge of these institutions, what I have to say has broad enough implications that there will be useful nuggets for many people: parents, students, school personnel, former students. Much of what I do say is anecdotal, personal. I am not a social scientist. I do not have the broad data to make solid conclusions about education or parenting.

I am a student of history, a teacher of history; however, I am not an historian. I have no PH.D. I have taught US History, including the Advanced Placement class, European History, Ancient History, Geography, American Government, electives on Hitler and Nazi Germany for nearly 30 years, Russian History, and, more recently Western Philosophy. I have taught 7th through 12th graders, although only juniors and seniors with a smattering of sophomores for the last ten years. I have coached soccer, basketball, golf and baseball. I have lived in boys' dorms, a girls' dorm, in my own mortgaged house, and in school housing. I have taken school trips to Outward Bound programs, Germany and the USSR.

In short, I have some experience and some experiences.

After 33 years as a teacher, 9 ½ as a Dean of Students, I am on a bit of a break. I have a sabbatical during the 2nd half of the 2001-02 year, and it is the first year after 32 consecutive years in the classroom that I am not teaching. I decided that I would discipline myself to try to write enough for a book during my sabbatical. A major part of the reason I asked to take the sabbatical this year, after actually having been awarded it ten years ago, was that my wife was in her third year of a Masters in Social Work program. We had 2 small children, now 6 and 3, and juggling two major commitments while doing an adequate job of parenting was going to be a struggle. So I asked for my sabbatical so she could finish her studies, and then next year we would adjust. I expect to return as the full-time Dean of Students. Part of this book will be to explain what that job means.

I have experience, occasional insight, and a modicum of wisdom. Sometimes the American experience blends into the human experience, sometimes the reverse. The same is true for me personally.

I hope to identify themes that will connect the various chapters. The anecdotes, the philosophizing, and other people are in the book because of the connection to me. There is some fiction, some editorial modification of people and events, no names of students, and few names of other adults. Several emails are included in the book. I have copied them as they arrived rather than try to edit them. The flavors of their contents are reinforced by their styles, sometimes reflecting haste and sometimes simply ebullience or ire.

Two small pieces of fiction appear near the end: The Gift and The Model. They reflect my attempt to describe a boy and a girl who have successful high school experiences, negotiating the hazards and pitfalls that affect them and consume others. I have seen many successful students, watched many grow into that role while others have maintained it all the way through. Nevertheless, I believe every student experiences some angst, some failure, some temptation that is overcome, some doubt; even the most outstanding are not perfect. I want the reader to know that the kinds of kids in those two pieces are representative; however, they are not real people.

Essentially all of us have been to school, most of us to several, some for more years than they want to believe. Some people remain at school as teacher, or as staff member in some other capacity. Some get re-involved as parents of the next generation of students. We all know that school is more than a place where we learn some academic skills. We learn about friendship, about communication, about rules, civility, success and failure. We learn from our teachers, from ourselves, from our peers. We learn from older students, and many times from younger students. We all have memories, from the very good to the horrific.

I have been in schools for more than 50 consecutive years. Most of what I have to say is about the last ten and where all of us are right now. Perhaps like Star Wars, there will be both prequel and sequel.

THE DEAN

Dean is a four-letter word. While it is not always clear what the term means, my title at the school is Dean of Students. We also have a Dean of Faculty and an Academic Dean.

One of the earliest definitions of Dean was a senior member of a monastery overseeing ten monks. Fortunately, that does not apply to me.

It is also a definition of a senior member of a male group (female version: doyen), it is in my case a side effect of constancy with one employer.

As Dean of Students, I am essentially in charge of discipline, another of those elements of the definition of Dean. Dean of Discipline. Dean of Dress. Dean of Issues Other People Want to Avoid. That sounds too much like a march to martyrdom, and martyrdom is not my goal.

In fact, I really like my job. Most people do not understand how anyone could be or want to be a dean in a school of teenagers, and the turnover rate in most schools is rapid. My predecessor lasted two years, but his predecessor had the job for fifteen years, albeit sharing it with two others for much of that time (Dean of Women, Dean of Day Students). I now have two Assistant Deans, an expansion that reflects the amount of work to be done. We work well together, have the same general philosophy, can agree to disagree, and appreciate that while there is collegiality there is also a hierarchy. And I, too, have to report to a higher power; actually, more than one.

One of the roles I relinquished when I became Dean was coaching. Although I initially taught two sections of history and lived in a dorm for my first three years as Dean—all a bit hard to believe ten years later—I did give up my time on the athletic field. I ended as varsity baseball coach and girls' varsity soccer coach, but had at times been the boys' varsity basketball coach, golf coach and varsity assistant and JV coach for several sports; a typical boarding school career.

When asked if I missed coaching I now do not hesitate to say no. I like now to contrast that role with my Dean role, and while I fully appreciate the time and both physical and emotional energy that goes into the role of coach—especially varsity coach—I know I struggled with the idea of winning and losing. I hated losing, not in the sense that I was a sore loser, but rather in the sense that I questioned what I did or did not do, agonized over all those losing seasons (I managed to have seasons when the soccer and basketball teams won no games). I like to think I won with grace, lost with dignity, knowing that there were moments when neither was true. I subscribe to the philosophy that it's not whether you win or lose, it's how you play the game, but sometimes the practice of that philosophy does indeed get forgotten. In short, I am glad to be away from that struggle.

And the Dean's job is easier?

In the sense that I am constantly looking for what in the business we call win/win situations, I usually do not have to deal with winning versus losing. Certainly there are instances when I felt a loss or a win, but the loss was usually a greater sadness than a personal responsibility. I often second-guess myself, but I have a more optimistic outlook on looming problems or even crises than I did when I was coaching. I think I watched the clock and the scoreboard too much as a coach. But in dealing with people, adolescents especially, the clock and scoreboard are not important. The loss of a student in the community is often sad for the student, parents, and the community. However, it usually is best for all, and the long-term possibilities for growth as well as the recognition of that painful process of loss reflect a sense of optimism I could not always feel after a team loss.

The struggle for me is the attempt to balance what is good for the individual versus what is good for the community. Usually, I am not dealing with criminals, though there may be crime involved. I am dealing with kids; the crime is less important.

I would characterize myself as a student's Dean; that is, I am much more willing to take the student's view or side in a fuzzy conflict. Sometimes I am wrong, but the result of my being wrong is less a negative consequence than the value of being right when I bet on the student. The community goes on, loss of student notwithstanding. The student, however, may not recover for a long time, and conceivably not at all.

Several years ago a popular book title created good discussion: Hilary Rodham Clinton's *It Takes a Village*. When children are raised in a narrow framework of just parents, or more problematic still—of a single parent—the community suffers in the long run. Children need not only to learn how to read and write and do arithmetic; they need to learn to be social beings, to develop people skills that will serve them in the workplace as well as in the general community.

I live and work in a kind of village. I am not touting the village as a model that we should re-institute around the country. We live in a big world, a diverse place that cannot possibly be reduced to a microcosm of a village. A village can be small, confining, stultifying. Working in the same village where I live has drawbacks. We talk about the goldfish bowl effect, the insularity, the elite nature of this particular village. But I like to walk to work, to be able to call upon a number of different experts by first name (librarian, dishwasher, Headmaster, plumber), to know my neighbors.

My village focuses on adolescents, several hundred of them. Part of our—and I try to make it even more specifically "my"—job is to awaken them to the reality of living in a village. Adolescents can learn good manners from the carpenter, friendliness from the secretary, humor from the math teacher.

But it can be a real challenge when that sixteen-year old has arrived not having much experience with those values and practices. It takes the village to teach all those characteristics, and it takes years to inculcate and to practice them.

Character education has been the focus of discussion more recently after having been consigned to the dustbin of school programs. Honesty, respect for self and others, tolerance, overall ethical behavior—these are issues for the village. School is an essential part of the village, and in my case it is the reason for the village. The quadratic equation, the Dred Scott decision, and the periodic table are in the long run less important than character education, but it is easier to teach them, although the historian in me wants to argue about the Dred Scott decision.

When a seventeen year old boy sees his roommate's new shirt and asks to borrow it for the big dance the next night, we would all understand where that impulse comes from. When the roommate says no, we would respect that as well. When the seventeen year old takes it anyway because the roommate is away for the weekend, leaving the tags on so he can return it to the closet after he is done, we have a situation that can generate some strong feelings.

The village will scratch its collective head on this one and feel this student does not belong here. We have invited him into the village, now we want to send him out. Our village will certainly be a better place without this individual who entered this special village without, what we would consider, the appropriate training. Can we, or should we, try to "fix" this student? What if this instance is on top of something else worthy of serious response?

The village has a variety of responses to the individual. Centuries ago expulsion from the village was indeed harsh, because each village was almost a separate world. A person could simply not move into another village. If the individual had been deemed enough of a threat to the safety of the villagers and forced to leave he could be declared outside the law, in the English countryside anyway, an "outlaw". What other village would want to include such an individual?

In the 21st century we have community responses, sometimes involving rehabilitation, sometimes simply incarceration, warehousing the unwanted in large, well-guarded facilities, protecting "them" from "us" and "us" from "them". Out of sight, out of mind.

In school villages, we have an impulse, not abnormal I think, to rid ourselves of those that are problematic, difficult, seemingly incorrigible. While it is difficult to imagine an adolescent as incorrigible, we can sidestep the issue by allowing that person to go to a new village, to start over with a clean slate. In fact, juvenile law often protects adolescents from their own past by sealing the transgressions from the eyes of the new village. Adolescents get a second chance.

In my school this second chance comes under the heading of Probation. When a student commits a Major Rule violation that student goes on Probation. A second offense while on Probation necessitates a meeting with the Discipline Committee for a recommendation to the Headmaster as to whether the student should be allowed to remain.

We usually give students a second chance for violations of drug and alcohol use. Many schools do not. Many schools differentiate between marijuana and alcohol because one is illegal for everyone while the other is legal for people over the age of 21. We generally treat those two the same way. Some other drugs, less common but more dangerous, we deal with on a case-by-case basis. However, possession of quantities of either alcohol or marijuana that we deem sufficient to be considered "for distribution" warrants Dismissal on a first offense.

Nevertheless, the second chance also for us involves specific prerequisites for continuation: professional evaluation, appropriate follow-up as recommended, and drug screening, The village is part of the solution to the problem; if the student cannot abide by the stipulations then the student must leave the village. At least the student is not an "outlaw".

One of the fundamental differences between the school or village and the parents is that the school can formally cut the ties with a student. Parents can never do that. We may Dismiss a student; we send the student home. The parents may send the student off to another school or into the greater world. But they will never *not* be the parents.

Sometimes my specific role seems to be to make the parents understand that the problem is their problem, not the school's. Increasingly since the early 1990's I feel that parents have been more involved and more willing to accept the responsibility of parenthood and take charge of the student. Sometimes they realize that the student needs to be with them rather than at a residential school. Sometimes they also realize that the student needs to be at a specific residential, therapeutic school to deal with emotional or substance issues. Coming to grips with the reality of what the child actually needs is a difficult process, and I have learned increasingly to utilize the expertise of psychologists and other mental health professionals to assist me. Nevertheless, there are still parents who resist the advice and the help, despite my and the village's attempts to educate them.

We had a very bright but also very lazy student. That profile is not often our most successful product. This particular boy had a high-powered father, or at least a father that thought he was. The boy had come from a therapeutic school where he had accomplished what he needed to. He was ready for the regular program.

Finally in his second year, as a senior, he achieved what I now think he really wanted—to be at home. Sadly, that was not what his father wanted. The only way he could get home was to be sent home by the school. That would happen only if he committed an offense worthy of at least suspension. So he blatantly committed such an act, and he made sure he got caught. He bought a bottle of vodka, drank enough to be noticed, admitted he drank, gave up the bottle of vodka, and knew he had to go home.

The father almost would not take him. We had to threaten legal action because he was the parent and we were not. Eventually, the situation was resolved and the boy went home, graduating from our school later in the spring.

I was inexperienced enough to nearly get brow beaten by the blustering father, and I had to call on the Head for help. Clearly, this was a sad situation that demanded a more therapeutic response, but the parental desire not to be part of the solution compounded the problem. He would like to have had somebody else fix it. Somewhere he had divorced himself from his village, and the village I was part of could not work on the roots of his difficulties.

While if I had had more professional therapeutic involvement and counsel I might have had a less difficult outcome, the unwillingness of the parent to work on the roots of the problem made an agreeable parting of the ways virtually impossible. I do not know where that student is now, but I do know that his successful adult life will not be fulfilled until both he and his father work on those fundamental problems.

The role of the psychologist or therapist in schools is growing steadily, and it should. The professional in that arena is not a panacea for adolescent problems by any means, but no longer is the therapeutic process looked at as witch doctoring. No doubt the general public as well as the adolescent community is still apt to view people seeing a therapist as somehow flawed, but that is increasingly public bluster rather than serious concern. Although 1972 is now a distant past, George McGovern had to sacrifice a Vice-Presidential candidate—Thomas Eagleton—because he had seen a psychiatrist. I suspect the same reaction would be true today, but politics lags behind good practice in many areas.

Schools have their lore, sometimes pure mythology, with quirky people at the center of it. An example from my experience is the long-time teacher who offered weighty pronouncements from time to time. One favorite: Anyone who sees a psychiatrist ought to have his head examined. In the 21st century this particular character probably would not be teaching any more (although a character on the *Boston Public* television show belies that generalization!).

The school psychologist or counselor can play a key role because that person can listen to students without having an agenda. The rule is that everything is confidential—not disclosed to parents, teachers, or administrators—unless: a) the student waives that confidentiality or b) the student is a danger to self or others. The counselor is supposed to be neutral. Any student who comes into my office to talk to me knows that I am the Dean of Students. I cannot take off that hat, even though I can listen with the hat on the table. The dorm parent is always the dorm parent, the teacher the teacher, the coach the coach, the friend the friend, dad the dad. Each person has a role, and regardless of how good a listener or how wise a person in giving advice, that role is always there. The psychologist is not supposed to bring that bias to the table.

My ability to work with the psychologist certainly influences my interaction with students. If I can funnel information to the Health Services personnel or to the psychologist directly, they can have a heads up if the student shows any inclination to want some advice or help.

Most adolescents love to talk; they just do not want to talk with their parents, or their teachers, or with anyone they feel is in authority.

Discipline is such a wonderful word. It has that ring of power to it, fear of punishment, threat of consequence, ability to control. And it is misunderstood.

Language is powerful, useful, and fun. I like utilizing words to teach. While immediately that sounds trite and obvious, I mean that I enjoy taking the individual word and using it for instruction.

Discipline comes from the same root as disciple. Christians would not think of Jesus' disciples as being punished or forcibly herded into a conspiracy to spread the Word. They followed eagerly, willingly. The words "learning" and "pupil" are meanings from the root origin of the word that grew into both discipline and disciple; but the first meaning now given in the dictionary is punishment. That's too bad; we have locked away a good meaning, allowing a brother to usurp the throne.

Although I sometimes see myself as Dean of Discipline, I prefer to see the word as rooted in "disciple". People should act feeling that what they do is the right thing. There is a popular acronym around: WWJD—What Would Jesus Do? This year I decided to secularize it a bit, and I have a sign on my bulletin board: WALDI—Would Abraham Lincoln Do It? Clearly that won't work for everyone, but if each of us had some little acronym that guides us in times of decision-making we would have fewer problems in our lives.

I have not yet trained the student body in WALDI, but I have been working on another formula for several years that is becoming commonplace in my school. R=C+C: Responsibility equals Choice plus Consequence.

My mother sent me a cartoon not long ago. The parent is

scolding the child, telling the child that if the unacceptable behavior continues he will have to live with the consequences. The child pauses, then asks: Do they have a pool?

My relatives: the Consequences.

We all make mistakes, and often those mistakes are considered rather than accidental. In the school setting, breaking the rules is usually done with understanding aforethought. If someone drinks alcohol, smokes marijuana, leaves the dorm after check-in, that person knows full well that the decision was made consciously. Granted, we have had some incidents that started out—and on a rare and difficult occasion ended—with a response like: I have no idea how that partially empty can of cold beer got under my bed. More frequently I have had to deal with the he said/she said scenario that has dead end staring me in the face.

But if we take Responsibility we can move on. I made the choice, I accept the consequences. We all make mistakes; if we did not we would not grow because we would not have pushed the limits, we would not have stretched ourselves.

Indeed, there are many instances when we suffer consequences for something that happened that we did not choose. If a student slipped on the ice going to class and had to go to the Health Services to check for broken bones, thereby missing the test that was administered, is there a consequence? Certainly. Would we allow the student to make up the test? Certainly. Should the student have been more careful in walking on the ice? Probably, but now we venture into that murkier area of Blame rather than Responsibility. We can move on; we should.

If a student smokes marijuana, he may get caught. The consequences are prescribed. Sometimes students (or their parents) are reluctant to accept those consequences (evaluation, drug screening), but they have given up that choice by making the previous choice. We do not mandate counseling or drug screening for every student, and philosophically we do not believe we should. (We might very well talk about the value of such a practice, but that leads me down to the path to another favorite word: authority.) The responsible person accepts the consequences and moves on, to where may not be clear, but the path will indeed be different than the one just followed. Robert Frost:

> Two roads diverged in a yellow wood,
> And sorry I could not travel both
> And be one traveler, long I stood
> And looked down one as far as I could
> To where it bent in the undergrowth;
>
> Then took the other, as just as fair,
> And having perhaps the better claim,
> Because it was grassy and wanted wear;
> Though as for that the passing there
> Had worn them really about the same,
>
> And both that morning equally lay
> In leaves no step had trodden black.
> Oh, I kept the first for another day!
> Yet knowing how way leads on to way,
> I doubted if I should ever come back.
>
> I shall be telling this with a sigh
> Somewhere ages and ages hence:
> Two roads diverged in a wood, and I—
> I took the one less traveled by,
> And that has made all the difference.

Of course, we cannot evaluate that path until we have trod it, but we always have different paths in front of us.

If a student smokes marijuana, he may not get caught. Is there a consequence when someone does not get caught? I rather enjoy that kind of discussion. It makes Discipline workable.

Success at school is measured in many forms: academic, athletic, artistic, social. Awards and ceremonies are regular. We hope almost everyone receives some sort of public recognition for a job well done, but we still have a meritocracy. And it is often subjective.

Towards the end of the year the faculty meets to vote on awards to be given at the end of the year. Academic departments have awards for Best Work in. . . . Most Improved in . . . . The Athletic Department does the same. We also have awards for Sportsmanship and Unsung Hero or Person Who Performed Beyond Expectations (10th or 7th or 12th Player award, depending on the sport). The Theatre has several plays a year, the music program concerts and recitals, the dance program a performance.

But the crowning achievement is for the senior boy and senior girl who are voted The Headmaster's Prize and the White Blazer. They reflect the traditions of the schools that existed before the merger of two single sex schools. They represent what the faculty think is the best of the class. Rarely are they unanimous choices, both because there are usually multiple nominees and because the recipients are teenagers, imperfect beings on the road to imperfect adulthood. But they do represent the faculty's earnest efforts to reward excellence as they perceive it.

I have become uncomfortable with the procedure recently, not for any specific reason, but just because I am comfortable with any of the several choices that are presented. So I have comfortably settled in to counting votes for the Academic Dean as he manages the process. However, that is not always so simple, counting hands that are raised barely above shoulder height next to the enthusiast whose stretched arm begs for double counting. When the vote is a one-vote difference, at least I can recount. And we have not had a Florida chad problem, although one year there was a demand for a revote a week after the prize had been decided. The winner was on Probation and had been suspected of being guilty of another crime but it was never proved. The original vote stood, to the distaste and dismay of some.

My own favorite, though, was a White Blazer winner who came mid-year as a sophomore, nearly left after one night prior to school even starting in January, got on Probation about a month later for leaving the dorm after check-in, and finished as an outstanding student-athlete. She went to a prestigious Ivy League school, played and captained a varsity sport, and graduated with a degree. And although I haven't seen her in a number of years, I would guess that she is still "regular person."

As the Dean, I had little if any impact on her becoming the White Blazer winner, and that award we all know is not an automatic ticket to success. It is recognition of something achieved, not something to be achieved. We all hope that one success will lead to another, but my choice of her story is that she was a solid kid with talent that had her share of burdens. She was not perfect, but she made a difference that people recognized. If we focused on her Probation as a sophomore and excluded her from consideration because we demanded flawless character from our Best Student, we would have chosen a less deserving nominee.

The onion has many layers of skin. Some we throw away, the best we utilize. I enjoy looking at the whole onion kid.

> *I can't believe it's been tens years since I was at [school].*
> *Thank you for everything you did for me during my post graduate*
> *year. . . . I learned quite a bit that year, and its taken me a long*
> *time to realize it.*
>
> *I am not proud of some of my actions while I was [there]. I*
> *apologize for the disrespect I showed to many of the faculty and*
> *students.*
>
> *I have been busy since . . . . I graduated . . . with a BA in*
> *History . . . , and was commissioned in the Air Force. The AF*
> *has sent me around the world a few times, and I am enjoying*
> *every minute of it.*

Teachers are wont to say that they gain more satisfaction from this kind of feedback than from pay, but which of us in any job wouldn't have tremendous inner satisfaction from such a response? Educators primarily deal with people rather than money or things, but that should not replace monetary compensation! Nevertheless, letters like this validate what educators do.

Other less positive views from time to time surface. I have a few, but the job of Dean leads to more of that. Sometimes they are phone calls:

*"I want to register my disapproval of the way your staff
and school handled the situation this past weekend and my
strong objection to punishing my daughter for what happened.
If you had called me directly on my cell phone instead of leaving
a message on my home phone we would have resolved this much
earlier. Instead you called my husband, who has had no contact
with my daughter for 6 months and has no responsibility in her
being at your school, either financially or emotionally. My
daughter was extremely upset that her father was called, and you
should not have called him. I knew where she was all the time,
but you did not contact me directly, and now she is being
punished, suspended from taking weekends or whatever. She
said she turned in her green sheet, but that it must have blown
away somehow, but she did slide it under the door on time, and
if I had known I was supposed to call earlier I would have. This
is the first time she tried to go away for the weekend, and I knew
where she was all the time, but you didn't call me, and then she
received a letter this morning, addressed to her father which
really set her off, that said she was being punished because she
missed a class while she was at religious services, and that is
simply not acceptable. Just because she has not done this before
she should not be severely punished. I am sure there were mistakes
on several fronts, but your school certainly has been negligent in
allowing this situation to happen!"*

Having been practicing informal therapy now for quite some
time, I held my words, tried to breathe calmly, and waited out the
urge to jump in to defend, to respond with righteous indignation,
to lambaste this irate and poorly informed mother. I knew that
listening and waiting was a better strategy. I silently thanked the
therapists I had seen work, the counselors that practiced their
listening skills, the wiser experienced pros who knew when patience
was truly a virtue. That part of me that wanted to fire back was
successfully leashed. When we ended our conversation perhaps 15
minutes later, the anguished and angry mother was able to laugh,

to apologize and to know that a lesson had been learned without cruel and unusual punishment.

I could never prove that the daughter didn't slide the green signout sheet under the door, despite the reality that the last person in the room that night was the cleaning person, who knows what the green sheet is for and would not have thrown it away; or that the first person in the room the next morning, at 6 AM before anyone else has arrived, was my secretary who would not have missed such a significant piece of paper. With no open windows, the idea of the paper blowing away or getting caught in someone's shoe had no credibility. But a parent would be hard-pressed not to believe the child. The idea of coming to a single truth had no chance of success. So we accepted multiple truths, learned a lesson, and believed that tomorrow would be better.

I can do that; many people cannot. And in my earlier years I would certainly have been in the latter group; there had to be a single truth or we could all go to hell.

While I have been the Dean, the following have occurred: a boy carved the word "homo" into another boy's back with a knife; several boys were expelled when they had an organized hazing and harassment program in the dorm which included beating other students with sticks; a boy videotaped an entrapment of a student in an attempt at an "outing" of his homosexuality. None of them happened at my school. Neither did the Columbine incident nor the attempted copycat incident in New Bedford, MA several years after that. But they could have.

Similar incidents have occurred during my watch, but they did not progress as far and they did not get the national press. We were both lucky and perhaps more proactive so they did not get to that level. But I know that we cannot for a moment be complacent or think that we have done all we could.

Hazing has earned a great deal of disciplinary attention in the last decade, and most people agree: "about time!". Not everyone, though. The group dynamic, particularly but not exclusively with young males, still has supporters or apologists that believe hazing toughens up the younger members and prepares them for the realities of the adult world.

While not many victims will have permanent and visible scars on their backs, many will have unseen emotional scars, and some of them will reveal the consequences later. Much of it will be in the form of violence, to self or others.

On one occasion we had to work with the basketball team, who had shaved the head of a young member while away at a tournament. He had "agreed" to have his head shaved, but his parents were not pleased. They were not happy with his "consent," and the school was confronted with an uncomfortable situation.

Consenting to be a victim of hazing is self-contradictory. The football team had a similar rite that took place in the locker room and shower facility after practices. Victims did not come forward directly, and only through rumors did we discover some of what was going on. The threat of more serious action by the school ended what had been a "tradition." The girls' hockey team had an alcohol-focused party in the dorm prior to going away for a tournament. Again there was pressure to participate, to bond with the other members of the team. Any of these incidents, and many more, could have escalated or resulted in far more serious conclusions. And they could have happened in any school, residential or village, private or public, religious or non-denominational.

These are not situations that people seek to deal with because they like to; they are situations that we must deal with because they happen. They are endemic and pervasive, and yet we can find success in our dealing with them.

ON DUTY

People at my school often ask me if I am ever not "on duty," because whenever I am on campus students and adults alike often approach me for advice, comment, or expectation of action. An example of the latter: I am in the dining commons, with my 6 year old and 3 year old, and someone approaches me to do something about the student who is wearing a scarf on his or her head. At our school, head covering except for religious reasons is not allowed in classroom buildings, the chapel or the dining commons. So I have at times had to make crucial decisions on headbands, ribbons, Burger King crowns, etc., both on the spot and after sometimes thoughtful and often tendentious discussion about the decline of our school ethos or western civilization or youth in general. This might take place during the salad course, while I am getting an ice cream for the kids, or while I am returning my tray of dirty dishes to the conveyer belt. At least I do not have to worry about breaking the wine glass.

Or a student might approach me to ask me to excuse some penalty for a transgression that was "unfair." Now "fair" and its antonym are my least favorite words. I know what we all mean when we say we want something to be "fair," but in practice it means what an individual wants as opposed to not wanting. It was not "fair" that he was issued a penalty when he was wearing his hat in the dining commons; after all, he was on his way out, or he forgot, or he was just going to be there a minute, or both hands were occupied. So it is either unfair to the student for receiving the penalty or unfair to the adult for retracting the penalty. Meanwhile, my pasta is getting cold.

And of course Mr. Bell's crowning achievement also awaits my response. Parents have called at dinner time at my home, students have called after I have gone to bed, the dining staff have called when they arrived at work at 5:30 AM to find all the chairs missing.

Email with all its own difficulties is not shrill and does not demand an immediate response. The importance of some reflection, not necessarily two weeks' worth which is sometimes the length it takes for some people to respond to a request or a question, is crucial. I find it quite easy to make a mistake with a quick response, and I have to resist that temptation. I do not like things left undone.

Partially it must be my fault because of the kind of person I am, but partially it is the nature of the job. The Dean has, I think, a responsibility to the larger community. The 9-5 concept, or even the whole day on whole day off concept, does not apply. Somewhat like a full time parent, the Dean has to be available always. Nevertheless, just as the parent must—and I should emphasize that word "must"—take time for self to remain emotionally and psychologically healthy, so too the Dean must guard some time for regeneration and reflection. Striking the balance is the challenge.

My office has evolved rather significantly in the last decade. At first, I had my experienced secretary, I lived in a dorm, I taught two classes, including an Advance Placement section of US History, and a senior elective. After three years, I moved from the dorm to a recently renovated school-owned house (coincidentally named The Birthplace), became a parent, had an Assistant. Later, I dropped the US History course, and the school moved to elevate the position of Activities Director, originally a part-time position, sometimes staffed by a young person right out of college, to an adjunct of the Dean's Office with the additional title of Assistant Dean in charge of Residential Life.

Parkinson's Second Law—work expands according to the time available to fill it—seems to fit well with the Dean's job. While I would seem to have more time I certainly do not feel like I have less work. Certainly some of the emphasis shifted: working more with my assistants, becoming part of the Administrative team, thus attending additional meetings, working more with the Health Services personnel, having 2 children. Additionally, the computer as both a useful tool and taskmaster, gives us more opportunities to organize and follow information and requires us to spend time doing so.

While I may be spending less time personally with students, the other deans have compensated more than enough with their time with them. The result has been an increase in efforts to deal directly with students. We have both broadened our contacts and had the opportunity to have even more depth.

I think also that I have spent more time communicating with parents.

Parenting, no doubt, is hard work. There are probably few—if any—parents who have not had self-doubt about the job they do. I am too strict. I am too lenient. I pay too little attention. I am too involved. I second-guess my decisions, question my effectiveness, experience angst that I have not been perfect. Perhaps my head was right and my heart wrong, or vice-versa.

And yet we cannot entirely predict the outcome of the child we created, who will turn first into an adolescent and then into an adult.

I constantly remind myself that I am not perfect, and by extension that my children will not be perfect. I can only hope that my good faith in trying to be a good parent will result in an outcome that will make me happy and proud. As I learned once—and have often repeated in meetings with parents—our job as parents is to give our children roots and wings. If we have grounded them well in the fundamentals of decency, of humaneness, of empathy, then those roots will enable the adult to flourish. But at some, perhaps painful, point we have to allow them to fly from the nest, to experience their own freedom and self-ness. They will take their roots with them, replant them in their own space and time, and start the regeneration of the human process. This is a biological imperative, even if it does not always come to fruition to individuals.

As the Dean, or parent, in a school of several hundred adolescents, I cannot plant roots in the students who matriculate. That has already been done. As we are wont to say in school, the acorn does not fall far from the oak. Often I feel I am working hardest with the oak—the parent who cannot believe the child could do such a thing (when a situation has occurred that has put the student at risk of suspension or dismissal). I am not a family therapist or a psychologist. But I am increasingly aware when one of those professionals and experts needs to be part of the solution. Fixing roots of an unhealthy plant is a difficult task. They are not visible, they have been unhealthy for a long time, and simply trimming the above ground limbs will not fix the plant.

I often opine: parents should not send a child to school and expect us to fix him or her; the student has been broken for a long time. A new environment, rigorous program and stern discipline will not be enough. That's like trimming the limbs. It's not that schools or new environments cannot effect a substantial change; they can. But if parental or school expectation is for a quick remedy then the prognosis for success is not good.

I am occasionally amazed, always pleased, when I have a report from my own children's school or another parent that my child is well-behaved or polite or thoughtful. I do indeed see that positive behavior at home, but I occasionally see its opposite and I revert to my doubts and frustration and sometimes anger. Will I survive parenthood! But perhaps I am doing well-enough, not perfect, but well enough.

As Dean, I am most often dealing with the process of the growth of wings in adolescents. They want to fly, sometimes too far, sometimes too fast, sometimes not far enough. They experiment, test limits, test the patience of the adults. My job is nest manager.

My first weekend of being Dean of Students in September of 1992 touched the roots and wings issue literally as well as figuratively. The call to the walkie-talkie came at about 11:15 PM when the dorm parent reported a new sophomore missing, failing to check in by 11 at the dorm on Saturday night. Nobody had seen the boy for several hours. We decided to wait until midnight in case he might have conveniently thought check-in time was 12, as it was for juniors and seniors. Shortly after 12 I received the call that reported him still missing. It was time to call the parents.

One small immediate consolation was that he lived in Seattle so it was three hours earlier there, not as horrendous a time for the reception of this kind of phone call—I hoped!

No answer.

I decided not to leave a message because it just seemed more appropriate to speak directly to parents about their missing child.

About 1:15 I called again. The mom answered, and as I was starting to explain the reason for my call she interjected that she thought it might be me. Her son had, a short while earlier, walked in the door.

All of us were a bit nonplussed, but we were all relieved. The saga was repeated for my edification.

The boy had decided that afternoon that the school was not right for him, and he decided to go home. He went to the airport, bought a ticket on his credit card, and boarded the plan to Seattle. When he got on the plane, he said, he had second thoughts and wanted to get off. The staff would not let him, and he winged westward for home, spending a number of hours pondering his decision, and no doubt his fate.

Both he and his parents agreed that he had made a huge mistake, and the next day he was back on a plane heading east, returning in time for evening study hall.

He had exercised his wings, checked on his roots, and when he found they were firm he re-exercised his wings.

Three years later he graduated, not without other adventures and deep pitfalls in the process, but he knew that he had made the right choice by coming back east.

I call this event Sleepless in Seattle; a unique start to my career as Dean.

In fact, though, the Seattle saga was not my first task. In addition to preparing for the opening of school by planning, writing summer letters, working with colleagues over the summer, I had many initial contacts with both students and parents.

Our school is a tobacco-free campus, and when students are caught smoking they have a penalty. That policy has evolved and expanded over the years while we all struggled with the issues. However, it is a clear policy.

New students and their parents met at 5 o'clock on the first Sunday night when all the new students arrived on campus for the registration procedure. Immediately after that meeting, which lasted perhaps 45 minutes, one of the new students was caught smoking behind the chapel and reported to me.

Within a day I learned that this boy, a post-graduate who was 18, had the previous week been released from an in-patient program where he had been placed to recover from heroin addiction. The parents had not informed the school. They hoped that the in-patient program, a new environment, a college-prep focus, and a commitment from their son would get him through the initial difficult period. It was clear he had replaced one addiction for another and would not be able to abide by our expectations. He left before classes even began. He was not ready for his wings. I never knew what his roots were.

Most of the students with solid roots end up passing through the school smoothly and without memorable incidence. Some never seem to have gotten into any trouble: no unexcused absences, no other minor rule violations, and no Major Rule violations. Some get through with a few glitches, hardly anything out of the ordinary in a teenager's progress through the difficult years. And it seems to me that the ones who have the solid roots have little trouble getting back on track and even forgetting that they even made mistakes.

There are wonderful examples of kids who went through their careers with one significant misstep, each when they were freshmen, significant enough that they went on Probation and yet virtually forgotten by themselves years later. Perhaps they remain in my memory bank recall because I knew them personally better than some others and because I came into contact with their parents more frequently. It is not hard to pay compliments to the parents in these cases.

One girl was particularly prominent in her class: good student, class officer, athlete. She never seemed to be even on the fringe of difficulty, but she did have one, somewhat amusing incident that landed her on Probation. It apparently has turned into a good family memory because it demonstrated a flaw when she herself thought she would not and did not make mistakes; a gentle spice of humility to add some tang to life soup. This is her story.

We had had a number of minor transgressions of girls being in boys' dorms and vice-versa, not with any malevolent intent, but just to push the envelope of the rules. Several had been reprimanded rather than put on Probation, but in this case the Discipline Committee decided that there had been enough of this kind of transgression, and a firm message would get the attention of the student body.

In our school the Discipline Committee includes students, who are elected after a self-nomination process, and faculty members who are chosen now by the Chair of the Committee, although for many years they also were elected by their peers after a self-nomination process. A representative of the Dean's Office also sits on the Committee. Each Committee meeting, with different members of the pool chosen for each session, includes an equal number of student and adult representatives, usually three of each, plus the Chair, who votes only in cases of ties. The student in question appears with the adviser. After testimony and discussion, the Committee excuses the student and the adviser and votes a recommendation.

One day between classes this particular girl was coaxed to see a boy's tie collection (there were several students around); or perhaps she initiated the act; I don't remember exactly where the first step was made. The boy's room was just down the hallway from the common room in front of the dorm in the center of campus. She stepped into the room with the door open and several students present. A faculty member walked by and turned her in.

The Discipline Committee was eager to handle a case like this so rather than do something less than the letter of the law I forwarded it to the Committee. They recommended she be placed on Probation. She was. It was the only difficulty she had in her four years in the upper school.

Whether this was a turning point to make her (and others by the example) realize the seriousness of the commitments to our rules certainly would be open to discussion. Now, having known her parents and her for a number of years, I do not doubt that her solid roots and support at home would have meant any different outcome in the long run regardless of what the school did. I doubt the incident did little if anything to inhibit her success at the school. I think she hardly remembers the incident and probably feels it is not even worth remembering, except that it is a good opportunity for others in her family to bring her off any high post she may wish to sit on to declaim her right to deification. It recalls the Sermon on the Mount where Jesus warns his audience not to try to take the moral speck from a neighbor's eye without first removing the log from their own.

The second girl had a more serious incident, this time with marijuana at a trip to Fenway Park. She got "busted", and although it was a long time ago in her life it may have been more a pivotal point than checking out a tie in a closet. But the same family support and concern, the same established family roots, the same commitment to doing the right thing made it possible for this girl to graduate in much the same fashion as the previous one. And she will need no teasing to keep her on the reality track. I was almost embarrassed when I brought it up to her one day because she thought it was such ancient history that she was appalled that I remembered it. However, my intent was to have her view of it from the perspective of a blossoming adult knowing she had made a mistake. At that moment, however, she did not want to see it that way! Maybe later she will want to talk more about it, but it would not surprise me if she just would like it to be buried to avoid any embarrassment. But I like the story because she turned out to be such a terrific kid.

When we are dealing with groups of people, we certainly need to be aware of our unconscious stereotyping and bias. The two stories I just related involved the traditional nuclear family, father and mother and siblings, but solid roots come from families where there is only one parent, divorced parents, families from far away and near, many siblings and none. Some families are regular churchgoers, some not at all, some have wealth, some have few discretionary funds. But all the successful families have provided support, attentiveness, and love.

Clearly it is more difficult for an institution like a school to inculcate those qualities. They are personal qualities, qualitative rather than quantitative, and schools cannot provide qualitative accounting; people do. Good schools must insure that the systems they have established are workable and effective, but the people that work in and with those systems must also have the time and energy and skill to work with adolescents. And what is the compensation for that effort?

To some degree the question relates to the more philosophical question of what is the reward or compensation for being a parent? Why do people have children? Certainly in the early part of the 21st century the simple biological imperative can be circumvented and frequently is, but people do not have children for investment purposes; the long term benefits are not listed in the ledger book next to the costs for orthodontists, fast-food restaurants, and college.

Good parents are such because they participate in the journey of growth with their children. Do good educators follow the same path with the teenagers in their charge?

I have often talked about altruism in my classes, and I view altruism as equivalent to cutting something in half over and over again; I can theoretically never get to zero. I do not believe anyone is truly an altruist; people are more or less altruistic. Mother Theresa, a good model for altruism that stood out at the end of the last century, gained spiritual satisfaction from her work. She had compensation: she felt good about what she did.

I like to think I get some of that compensation for my work. Sure, I live in a nice house, can walk to work, have my grass cut and snow plowed, do not have utility costs or maintenance fees. I even get paid a pretty good salary. But I also seem to be a reasonably stable, sensible, contented man who has his own personal struggles to go with the stress of the job. But I don't think I complain about the job. I like it; most people would not.

Perhaps I have enough altruistic sentiment in me to enjoy the satisfaction of having someone else succeed because I have helped. Perhaps the psychologist might say that this altruism is the obverse side of a coin on which the other side is masochism. The teenagers and parents who have less success while the former are traversing that rocky time passage may be out of balance with the altruism/ masochism coin. Some of the words we often hear about teenagers are: selfish, spoiled, self-centered, egocentric, solipsistic, narcissistic. They all center on the preeminence of "me;" so too with the parents.

I remember an ad I saw that struck me as emphasizing a counterproductive effort for a good family. It showed the father climbing out of bed at 4:30 AM, quietly going down the stairs and nearly tripping over a toy that he then carefully removed from harm's way. He was on his way to work, a stockbroker who would be ahead of the crowd when the financial markets opened, taking care of business for his clients that would make his own family more financially secure. The message was that the company worked hard for the benefit of their clients, and that the people who worked at the company put in long hours and heavy commitment so that many could benefit. And I thought: when did dad see his children? Was money going to compensate for the absence? I suspect that I was not the only one who cringed at the ad; it did not last long.

My report card on my own dad-ness will have many more checkpoints before I can have anything like a final report, and even that will be like the cutting in half project. At least my own shortcomings will not be physical absence in the early years.

Residential schools have an inherent challenge because dads and moms are not present. The schools have to provide substitutes, and they are never the same. Sadly, they can occasionally be better than the real parents but that is not their goal. That happens when the adults in the school are caring and involved and the parents are both physically and emotionally distant. Physical distance does not have to be a major problem, especially now that we have effective instant communication by telephone and computer. However, the technological communication is not adequate substitution for emotional closeness.

The other danger in the residential school is the substitution of the peer group for the parental influence. That is an area where we have worked hard in the last decade. Peer support is wonderful, but the direction of the peer efforts is crucial. We talk about peer pressure a great deal, and without positive adult presence that peer pressure can be misguided and harmful.

I think one of my duties as Dean is to make sure the peer pressure is monitored and influenced. I can do that more effectively if I have access to the peer group, and I can only hope to do that by having a combination of empathy and a trustworthiness that I will maintain my adultness while "hanging out" with the teenagers. They do not want me to be a teenager. They want me to be the adult, in this case the Dean. They know my role, and they want me to play that role. At the same time they appreciate that I will at least listen.

Adults make mistakes when they attempt to be a "friend" of the teenager. My advice to the adults is to be friendly while recognizing that an adult can never be a friend. A friend is a peer. Adults and teenagers are not peers. More often than is articulated, teenagers do not respect adults who do not keep an appropriate distance. That distance varies according the personality of each party; some that are too distant are ineffectual, equally ineffectual are the ones that are too close.

THE VILLAGE

I have decided to use the term "village" in this book equivalently with the words "school" and "community". They are not the same, each with several meanings, each having different contexts. But I am going to play off the success of a United States Senator who, as First Lady, had some success with the title and the context for it. I want to emphasize the importance of personal interaction by people who live, necessarily, with other people.

Much of the success of the United States has been attributed to the emphasis on individualism and independence. These are both valuable philosophic tools, but they are inadequate as full philosophies. The same is true with the concept of village; we should not reside in villages without having interaction with people outside the village and with other villages. Although I am drifting into the realm of political philosophy, I do think it important that I place my school, my community, and thus my village, in the context of a greater environment. I am neither an ardent nationalist nor a fervent internationalist. I believe in the place that I live and the necessity of connecting it to other places.

Within this place, which I sometimes refer to as the village, each individual deserves the respect of others and the opportunity to develop the potential inherent in the being; yet not at the cost of hurting someone else. I do not believe that in order to climb the ladder of success we have to step on other people's fingers on a rung. Competition is not at odds with cooperation, and independence is not at odds with interdependence.

Within the village ordinarily there is a school, and I mix my metaphors when I equate them here. In my context the school is the village, but there are more than just teachers and students. In my context the school is the community in terms of what we all have "in common." We share space; we share a common philosophy; we share differences.

Many people do not stay in this particular village very long, which differs from the traditional sense of village. We have the image of the traditional idea of the village where people are born, grow up, work, and die; that concept of village is diminishing rapidly as we start the 21st century. In this particular village, the majority of people in any one year spend a maximum of 4 years actually living there, a maximum of 6 years using the village as a school and community beyond the home, which lies in another village. We might have boarding students for 4 years and commuters for 6; our 7th and 8th grades are only for day students.

Even the adults in this particular village are apt to move after a few years. We recently had a number of village elders retire after working here in excess of 30 and sometimes 40 years, but that was an unusual time. In the traditional village, they stayed on and were part of the community; that continuation is not part of our particular village. Our village has a more specialized function: to serve as a setting where teenagers can prepare to leave the village. I think we should hope more that they attach themselves to another village so that they can have a sense of community, a sense of belonging. Individualism and independence should prepare them to reconnect, not disconnect.

The village can also be a small place, and when people live and work in close proximity the pressures to conform are stronger than in the larger context of a city. In the urban environment, an individual can find anonymity, can escape, consciously pursue aloneness, or inadvertently find loneliness. The village can ostracize individuals. In my village it happens as well, though I think less frequently than some other places where people can act small and be smug about it. Some leave the village with feelings of bitterness.

Do you mind not sending me any more emails? I don't like hearing about stupid class stuff from you since i technically don't graduate . . . . remember? Plus i really don't like even thinking that you are in charge of this kind of thing since these updates just remind me of how much I

*hated you in high school. Please take me off the list serve and don't
contact me anymore.*

I think this kind of response is sad, and the former student
who was trying to keep connections with the bitter one felt
saddened by the sentiment. The bitter student had had trouble in
his tenure with hazing, alcohol, and dishonesty. One result was
not graduating, but the sense of the email reflected a lack of
resolution on his part, a continuation of blame rather than
acceptance of responsibility.

Other people have moved out under unhappy circumstances,
and I always hope there will be reconciliation. Smallness is not a
healthy quality in an individual, and we work fairly hard but not
always successfully to overcome that.

It is probably harder when I am more directly involved because
I am so connected to the village, so much a part of it for so many
years. And yet I have had good conversations with some students
who left under difficult circumstances. Some perhaps were simply
pro-forma or polite conversations that did not attempt to
completely acknowledge the past; some were genuine attempts at
reconciliation. I have, for better or worse, made the village a key
component of my life, and I know I am not the norm.

Another inspiration for this emphasis on village is the title of a
book: *Bowling Alone*. This study was the result of a social scientist
collecting a great deal of data and then putting it together. I, of
course, am gathering very little data and a fair amount of personal
experience so my inspirations are eclectic. The concept behind the
title is that Americans are spending less time in community activities
and more time alone.

The traditional village would have had its equivalent bowling
alley. Play as well as ceremony would have been bonding activities
that held the villagers together. I do not think the statistics in the
book are surprising, but we citizens do not usually reflect a lot on
statistics as we go about our lives. Americans do seem to feel that
there is something lacking in their lives, even when satisfaction, as
evidenced by polls, seems high. That sense is also inherent in a

society that places a great deal of faith in individualism; aloneness is a byproduct.

If, on the other hand, we achieve a state of satisfaction, how much of it has resulted from the process of striving for that satisfaction? If we do not have to strive any more then we will not be satisfied. We live for the moment knowing that tomorrow will in fact bring another moment. This is a conflict.

In my school as village we are both consciously and subconsciously aware of this conflict of process versus product. We feel that we have to keep placing goals in front of the teenagers to urge them forward, and then when we have deemed them ready we send them out of the village in a ceremony we call Graduation. Some students are more than ready to leave, some think they are but are not, and some are not but they go anyway.

The Graduation ceremony is usually well conducted, with that sense of formality tinged with excitement. There are speeches, awards, and then the presentation of that official document called the Diploma. Most are signed, but occasionally some are not. Maybe the student failed a course; maybe the parents had not paid the bill; maybe the individual had a disciplinary problem not yet resolved. We allow them to participate because the ceremony itself is an important part of the experience of moving on from the village, perhaps even more important than the actual diploma, which they can earn later.

What most often follows is the realization, finally, that the village is not totally theirs any more. As they walk through the line of faculty receiving congratulations and well wishes, the tears begin to flow, usually at a higher rate as they get towards the end of the line where the most senior members of the faculty have their place. There is a visceral recognition that, while they want to move on— new schools, new courses, new challenges, new friends—they have to say good-bye. It is not really a permanent good-bye, those come at a much more difficult moment in our lives, because they can return to visit, can communicate easily if they want, and have a permanent connection with their peers who are sharing the same moment. But for some it is the moment the emotional bond has been permanently changed. The village is now a "there" rather than a "here."

This sense of "there" and "here" pervades the life of the village. We see it in athletics: the rival team, the school we love to beat; we see it in what are called town/gown relationships with our neighbors; we see it in "weekends" when students go someplace else to be away from "here."

Sometimes the sense of "here" and "there" is a healthy development of a new perspective; sometimes it is decidedly unhealthy when people lack empathy and characterize those outside the village as "other." My experience as a history teacher has led me to bring some of that experience to bear as the Dean.

Since 9/11 the sense that Americans are doing less "bowling alone" has been a theme among many writers and commentators. Robert Putnam in his book *Bowling Alone* hinted that the country was ready for a new commitment to community, and then 9/11 occurred. How long the country can sustain this new sense of togetherness remains to be seen, but it is part of a cycle and the further we get from 9/11—unless there are significant new developments that directly impact the country—the more we will revert to the individualism that is part of the American fabric. It reinforces my belief that the strongest force for unity is having a common enemy. Unity and its spin-off community thrive on the duality of "there" and "here", of "us" and "them". Nationalism, that force within a country that bonds the nation—a group of people with a sense of common purpose—depends on the sense of "other", raises it to a fever pitch when the "other" can become the "enemy." Absent the "enemy," which has to be identifiable and visible, not just a philosophic or spiritual term, and the nationalism fades. However, in a strong country this nationalist force is always lurking.

The events of 9/11 had the same intensity in our school that it had in the broader context, and it had a profound impact on both the village and individuals in it. Our diversity raised other concerns; many of the international students were nervous and fearful that they would be cut off from their homes in Europe and Asia. Talk about going home, leaving the United States, was not uncommon; by February only one person had left for the that reason, and that was because her parents wanted her home rather than her wanting to leave.

We also had to deal with some sense of hostility that manifested itself in the stereotypes attached to individuals, but it was certainly less intense than in other places. We were spared the direct sorrow that many other schools had to contend with, but we knew of many instances where people in our school had lost loved ones and friends.

Nevertheless, our sense of community helped us through a difficult emotional period. Our Health Services personnel were of course professionally ready to utilize their skills. Moreover, the sense of willingness on the part of the adults throughout the community to lend support to the students, in addition to the support they had to have for their own families and friends, was noticeable. It was not necessarily because we as a community suddenly came together. We did have an all-school assembly followed by smaller groups facilitated by adult leaders, and while that was important, it was not as important as the pervasive spirit that predated 9/11.

That Tuesday was the first day of classes for us in the new school year. We had just finished an assembly introducing us all to the commitments ahead. The first class was starting. Like my generation remembering where they were when they heard the news and saw the pictures of John F. Kennedy's assassination in 1963, like the previous generation having the same experience with the events at Pearl Harbor in 1941, 9/11 will have that long-lasting impression for many.

As I write this we are in the midst of concern about sustaining the national effort to find those responsible for 9/11 as well as insuring that we are as protected as possible from future terrorist acts. While the icons of 9/11—Osama Bin Laden and Mullah Omar—have not been found, the threat of another terrorist attack has diminished. The government's efforts to expose and destroy the terrorist organizations and their members are ongoing, but people know that it may never be fully eliminated. If someone wants to commit an individual act of personal sacrifice and destroy something else in the process, it can still happen. It is increasingly difficult for an individual to do so, and it is more difficult now for an organization of self-sacrificing true believers to act in concert. But we sense that such a terrorist act is not impossible.

Yet the country has gone on with its life. Five months after Pearl Harbor the country was in a different mood than the United States is in early 2002. Five months after Kennedy's death the mood of the country was still fitful. Other factors, internal rather than external, were roiling that mood: civil rights, women's rights, and the Vietnam War. Perhaps President Johnson tried to sustain that national sense of commitment that was part of Kennedy's legacy by his War on Poverty, by the Civil Rights Acts, and by increased commitment to Vietnam. His attempts at creating that centrifugal force resulted in disunity rather than unity.

The same disintegration happened at my school, and the turmoil of the late '60's and early '70's ended with a merger with a girls' school—bringing coeducation to both—and some leadership changes accomplished by further divisive measures. The village was breaking apart; there was less sense of community, bowling alone seemed more representative of the lifestyle in the school.

The country had the conflicting forces of the Global Village and the Me Generation. While those are arbitrary phrases applied to a vaguely defined time, they have merit in having us think of broad terms rather than atomized incidents. My sense is that the Deans in the '60's and '70's were trying to hold the village together as it threatened to disintegrate completely. I certainly do plenty of reacting in my job in the 21st century, but the village has come back together and there is more of a sense that we all have to work to make the community act as one.

Putnam reintroduces us to a useful term: social capital. In our economic system, using resources, and particularly money, to invest in the future for development of even more resources, is a fundamental practice. In village terms, investing in good relationships with other people will bring increased personal involvement with other individuals and with the whole community. If involvement turns into commitment then the village has become stronger. If it is good for me then it is good for us. In contrast, if it is good for me and detrimental to others then the village is hurt. The discussion in the country, as I write, is focusing on the executives of a giant corporation—Enron—and the workers within the company. As the company went bankrupt, some seemed to have benefited financially while the vast majority suffered enormously. What Enron executives did was not helpful in adding to the capital of the village.

Without recognizing the appropriate social psychological terms, I think my school has moved towards being a stronger village because we began to value social capital in its core meaning.

> "By analogy with notions of physical capital and human capital—tools and training that enhance individual productivity—the core idea of social capital theory is that social networks have value. Just as a screwdriver (physical capital) or a college education (human capital) can increase productivity (both individual and collective), so too social contacts affect the productivity of individuals and groups.
>
> Whereas physical capital refers to physical objects and human capital refers to properties of individuals, social capital refers to connections among individuals—social networks and the norms of reciprocity and trustworthiness that arise from them. In that sense social capital is closely related to what some have called 'civic virtue'. The difference is that 'social capital' calls attention to the fact that civic virtue is most powerful when embedded in a dense network of reciprocal social relations. A society of many virtuous but isolated individuals is not necessarily rich in social capital."
> (Putnam, 18-19)

There is no equivalent 9/11 for the change in my school, though the historian in me wants to wait quite some time before giving 9/11 the same seat on the pantheon of events as Pearl Harbor and

THE DEAN: ON DUTY 47

the Kennedy assassination. My assumption of the Dean's position in 1992 is just a piece in the long run of events. I suspect, unlike Louis XIV, that "après moi, plus ca meme chose" will be more to the point than "le deluge." (After me, more of the same rather than the flood). I know that many of my friends who have retired recently have found that their connection in the village diminished quickly, particularly after a year away. By the second year away there are more than 200 fewer students that would have known the retiree. There would also be new faculty members who had no connection. No one of us in the village is indispensable. The village will continue, changed, but nevertheless continue.

Still, I have held the position for ten years, not worthy of Guinness and his Book of Records, but also not the norm for that position. Burnout or the allure of higher aspirations has most deans gone before a decade.

To this point, both my appointment and my tenure have been the result of unintended banking of social capital. By unintended, I mean I had not aspired to the job, and like most members of the teaching profession I looked with a jaundiced eye to "administration" anyway. But personal changes for me coincided with the opening of the job. I threw my hat in the ring, navigated the shoals of the interview process, and was offered the job.

The holder of the title two persons before me had held the job for 15 years. He had two assistants much of the time, subtitled Dean of Girls and Dean of Day Students. When he decided that he was going to retire, going back to teaching for one more year first, the community strongly wanted an outside person who would come in and "shake things up." The village was struggling with its identity, with its practices, and with its need for greater commitment to the residential component of the school. The man they hired, actually the fourth in line to be offered the job, came from another school and was required to live in the dorm to be able to get a feel for the life of the school. The village did not want someone simply to "administer," they wanted someone who would be familiar with the innards of the community life.

After one year, he decided that the second would be his last.

He wanted to move on to do social work; the discipline element in the life of a school was too draining and distracting. And it invaded his and his family's personal life.

In hindsight, I think also he did not have the social capital that would have made his life and his job coexist more smoothly. He made a positive impact in his two years, but the work drained him.

When I applied for the job, I think I realized that I had more social capital than I thought and more ability to do the job than I believed. Whether that is sustainable of course remains to be seen, and while I necessarily have lost a little social capital—a Dean cannot make decisions without making someone unhappy—I have gained additional capital, enough to sustain me for the immediate future and some of which may be helpful further along when I may need it.

I am not accumulating chits, filing away IOU's in a social capital investment center. Social capital, the way Putnam means it is, is not the "I'll do this for you if you'll do this for me" kind of reciprocity. In fact, in the village sense of community it is "I'll do this because it is the right thing to do and it will help all of us". Doing the right thing is a theme I can see in many chapters of this book, but it is not always easily come by. The "right thing" may not in fact be the right thing for some people. But I am not much of a gambler (is the village football pool that much of a gamble?), and I am not one to risk a great deal on a contentious issue. I always know there will be more contentious issues later on.

One of my former colleagues, who was also my immediate boss, was fond of telling parents that the expertise of the school was in knowing the students in breadth while the expertise of the parents might better be described as knowledge in depth. Our professional experience with many students and the nuances and varieties that they have brought to the village has given us insight into how adolescents deal with peers, problems, and parents. However, we certainly do not know the individual student as well as the parent does (usually!). The practice of an effective village brings these two kinds of expertise together.

Sometimes students simply do not want to be away from home. The parents may have had good reason to try to send the student off to a boarding school: lack of academic success or focus in school, unhealthy friendships or personal relations, a turmoil within the family (perhaps the parents are separating or divorcing), lack of opportunity in the home community, and many others. We do know, though, if the student genuinely does not want to be away from home he/she will find a way to return there. If we as a school can involve such students in our village they may change their minds. For that to happen the village must be open and eager to accept new members, the older members shedding the "other" label as quickly as possible.

Why would any parent send a child off to a boarding school? In the crucial teenage years when the influence of parents is falling precipitously and the influence of peers is rising concomitantly, placing a child where there are more peers and no parents seems more than counter-productive: it almost seems criminal!

The boarding school village does indeed have a challenge. Can we be better than the best set of parents? No. Can the best set of parents, living where their children are not getting the best set of challenges nor a good coterie of peers, do the best for their children by leaving them in a school system that is either doing them more harm than good or not helping them reach their potential? Can they give them to a school system that has a residential life program and a set of adults that can provide good substitutes for the home situation? What a challenge for a family!

And indeed, what a challenge for a school! I think we are up to it. I believe that the schools that do create a strong village sense can adequately replace a good family structure and can certainly outperform a poor family structure. I am familiar with a large number of successes of students who have created a positive, healthy, developmental relationship with the adults in our community. These successes make me believe this kind of village has a strong rationale for the future. No school should replace parents; yet, the reality is that a school occasionally needs to play the role of substitute. Good residential schools are not substitutes for families so much as they are villages where there are many adults participating in the growth of the teenagers.

Even the non-residential schools, public and private, have significant challenges in the process of educating. Teachers have complained for a generation about difficulties in getting the job done in the classroom. They are overloaded with paperwork, asked to do more in terms of individual attention to more needy students, and are frustrated with the poor behavior of many children. Parents have neglected many of the responsibilities of good parenting, and they have succumbed to the lure of television and now to computers to do more of their job. They have also been stretched with the material demands of a successful family: more goods necessitate more income. Both parents are now more likely to work, and thus they are not in the home either physically or emotionally for a much greater period of time during the week. Women are now freer to seek their own intellectual and social potential, but there is a cost to that. The stay-at-home mom is less a normal sight than it might have been certainly two generations ago.

I have a bias. We all do, and I try to keep aware of mine and not let it be in control when I need to make decisions. Judgments, rather than decisions, are more susceptible to bias, but I want to separate the two as best as I can. It is helpful when they are the same, but sometimes they are not.

My bias about families is that I believe two biological parents in the home and committed to and involved with their children's lives is the best opportunity for an emotionally healthy child to negotiate the teenage years and become a healthy and successful adult, however we wish to define success. Given that bias, I am well aware that such a scenario is not now the norm and that there are many successful young adults who have come from a different family scheme. Many adults who are parents, biological or not, single or with a partner, have done and will continue to do an excellent job of parenting. I have been the Dean of their children and have had opportunity for praise as well as concern.

The good village can compensate for the various weaknesses in families. A good school can serve the function of an extended family and can be available when the parents are not, either physically or emotionally. However, good parenting is certainly not the purpose of the public school system, and it is not included in the primary training of the teaching profession, though college programs have responded to some of that need over the last generation. In my school, every teacher has a degree in a subject matter. They are perhaps less trained in the methodology of teaching than many of their counterparts in the public system. They also do not have to teach students who are not preparing for college, do not have to struggle with daily discipline problems in the classroom, and can continue to be challenged intellectually in their own area of interest and expertise. But in a school where students have many more commitments, not to mention the fundamental nature of a residential program, the teaching and parenting that goes on is not only important, it is expected. Thus, we have to prepare our adults to be surrogate parents, and for some that is too much to ask and too much to sustain. The ones that remain and that are good are gems in our educational system. In my school they have tremendous success in the interior workings of the village. We need more than a few of them to make the entire village thrive, but they are present.

I have a responsibility in the village as the Dean to insure that this part of the education is running smoothly. While I work mostly with students in a variety of settings, I also have to work with adults, primarily in the residential program. On the nights when I am "on duty" I try to visit dormitories. Not only do I have an opportunity to see students—put a name to a face early in the year and just have a sense of who lives where on the campus—I can see how the residential system is functioning. We insist on a study time from 8-10 on school nights, requiring a quiet atmosphere and that students be in their own rooms. We also expect them in the own rooms after 10:30 for underclassmen and 11:00 for seniors. These are the rules arrived at by the adults long ago and enforced by the community leaders. There are penalties for not abiding by them. Parents have similar rules in their own homes, but sometimes I have the sense that parents are overwhelmed by their adolescent children who are constantly testing limits, using their increasingly growing vocabulary and intellectual training to argue, and wearing down the tired adults who have their own daily struggles. In some ways having an institutional set of rules as in a school or dormitory relieves the adults from having to negotiate and argue. It is easier to say: those are the rules of the school, not mine. The personal is dispassionately replaced by the institutional, helping the adults avoid the guilt and weariness.

The danger is that adults in the school community will simply use that institutional line to avoid taking any initiative instead of showing intelligent flexibility when it is appropriate. The foolish consistency as the hobgoblin of little minds frequently rears its head in institutions. Balancing the need for consistency with flexibility remains the challenge. If we forget the challenge is there or believe that we have conquered that challenge then we will certainly be blind to some serious issues.

There are a number of different points at which educators seek to foster growth. Just as there are different disciplines within the curriculum—math, English, history, foreign language, etc.—so too are there broader elements of education: cognitive, emotional, physical, creative. Teachers are trained in the first: the subject matter and how to learn it. They invariably work with the second, the emotional, because they see students as individuals with unique personalities and personal strengths and weaknesses. The physical and creative often get special attention from teachers trained in those areas, and there too the teachers work with individuals. Students grow at different rates in each of those areas and do not reach the same level of maturity in each of them at the same time. But we often expect them to.

A school with a residential life program has to be even more aware of the emotional growth component. The boy who is 6', 200 lbs and fourteen years old is still a freshman emotionally. The senior girl with Honors grades may have some serious emotional shortcomings that will impair her ability to succeed at the next level. The junior who has solid but not spectacular grades but who is emotionally one of the stronger students in the school will have a greater likelihood of personal success despite not matriculating at one of the elite colleges. Our ability to know these teenagers as individuals will make us more effective. In a village a large number of people will have knowledge and influence on teenagers. Insuring that those large numbers are people of quality, maturity, and empathy will make the village a better place. Also insuring that the teenagers in the community are positive contributors is important.

There is school and there is home. When those two are not synchronized and in agreement the potential for trouble magnifies quickly. I would argue that exposure to differences will enable a teenager more smoothly to negotiate the challenges ahead. Life is not scientific in the sense of a predictable outcome, but we can identify some elements that will almost insure failure: abuse, neglect, distress. Poverty certainly is another key element that inhibits many young people, and one that has much broader social implications because the gap between the poor and the middle class, never mind the rich, is widening rather than shrinking. When the personal baggage gets added to the social baggage the chance for success is pretty small. But my school does not have to pick from that selection. The ones that attend our school, even with their baggage, have a legitimate chance to succeed.

We often talk about potential students or new students having "hooks" that will connect them to some established activity in the school. We worry about students, bright as they may be, who have no obvious non-academic interests and no particular drive to develop them. Our community strives for multi-dimensional involvement because we believe that makes the village a better place. An individual must be willing to contribute to the good of the whole: if I grow and improve then so do those who come in contact with me. This is an example of the "civic virtue" that Putnam described.

The sense of connectedness in the village stems from individuals using their hooks and developing new ones. Another term that Putnam emphasized was "schmoozing." By this he means the practicing of interacting with other people in such a way that it develops social capital. We tend to think pejoratively of the term "schmoozing" as something that politicians do at social events to gain votes; but we probably vote more frequently for good schmoozers than poor ones so it has value in that arena.

Adolescents are probably not comfortable at schmoozing, which requires a self-confidence that is not yet fully developed in that group. Teenagers are still going through some important changes— physical, intellectual, social, emotional—that drive them to seek common ground among peers rather than new relationships that might be acquired through schmoozing. Schmoozing cuts across the breadth of the social part of the village. The depth part that individuals want to develop comes later. The element of breadth is where our school's expertise lies and where we can encourage all the positive aspects of schmoozing. These would include learning to communicate with people different from us, becoming comfortable with diversity, trying new activities, learning how to become socially confident. If such activity turns into political capital for some individual then that is an added benefit; and both our village and our larger society need political leaders.

This is not to say that we do not value depth or strive to achieve it. We call such depth excellence, and it can be manifested anywhere in the village and recognized beyond it. We have academic excellence: Honors, AP courses, Cum Laude society, a valedictorian, National Merit recognition; we have athletic excellence: trophies, team awards, All-League or All-New England or All-American recognition; we have artistic excellence, demonstrated by performances and shows; we have personal excellence as demonstrated by leadership. Few of these excellences come from schmoozing. What we also value are individuals who can cut across general categories like athletes, scholars, computer experts, artists.

When the theater or music director can recruit athletes to try a different method of expression, when the dorm parent can encourage a shy teenager to be a Proctor in the dorm, when an adviser can persuade the advisee to join the newspaper staff, then we can magnify our success. If the adults schmoze in the village, they demonstrate to the students that personal interaction has merit. It also sets a tone that is supportive.

Schools have increasingly been trying to develop leadership and responsibility by having programs that challenge kids to cooperate and reach out. A good example of this has been our efforts to have the Proctors participate in a ropes course program. This outdoor education component has happened sporadically for several decades. Nevertheless, it has helped recently with our student leaders to extend them, to get beyond not only their own peer group and dorm group but eventually to get beyond their own village. Is not schmoozing an attempt to build social capital and is not leadership training an attempt to formalize schmoozing?

Just as there is depth and breadth in our individual personalities, so are there different lines of communication and authority within the village. The village leader needs to be able to schmooze with the villagers and also be able to exercise the authority necessary to take responsibility. The good leader knows when to schmooze and when to act as the person past whom the buck does not stop.

So too with our students in the community. A student leader has to be able to communicate across the breadth of the group, perhaps more so when living in a dormitory. The student leader has to live among peers and act appropriately when something is wrong. I have watched the tough choices teenagers have made when they knew their peers were using poor judgment, which jeopardized themselves and others. In many ways if the village can resolve the problem and keep it in the village then it is not grist for some other mill, particularly the mill of the "others," outsiders like the press or neighbors or competitor schools.

Intervening is not the equivalent of covering up. If there is a problem within a team or a dorm and the team captains or leaders in the dorm can effectively change the behavior of the individuals and prevent further abuse, then the scarlet letter does not have to be attached and a witch-hunt does not have to ensue. However, if the student leaders collude with the miscreants then the outcome is going to affect the greater village.

When I have to work with students around an issue that involves truth, I remind them of the court where testimony is asked for the truth, the whole truth, and nothing but the truth. The first part means do not lie, the second part means do not leave out important details in an effort to obscure the truth, and the third part means do not lead the court on a wild goose chase following irrelevant information. Every day in court and in every television program dealing with court issues, lawyers and witnesses contest the second and third parts. Written into the 5th Amendment of the Constitution of the United States is the famous "taking the 5th" to avoid self-incrimination. "Taking the 5th" is legal and time-honored, yet we enshrine the three parts with a solemn hand on the Bible. Truth and justice are not always compatible, and just as individuals struggle with the conflict so do villages. What is kept within the village or within parts of the village and what is shared beyond the village are struggles that leaders deal with all the time.

Our student Proctors are not required to "turn in" wrongdoers. In some schools they are. Our Proctors are not allowed to collude, but they are not required to reveal. There is a difference. Knowledge is power, knowledge assumes responsibility, but knowledge also offers the choice of acting on it or not acting on it. It is not simple. Do the ends justify the means? Never, says one school of thought. Sometimes, says another. To the first group, I ask: then what does justify the means? To the second: what does not justify the means?

This is why villages need philosophers. And Poets.

XVII Nunc lento sonitu dicunt, Morieris

John Donne, For Whom the Bell Tolls

> PERCHANCE he for whom this bell tolls may be so ill, as that he knows not it tolls for him; and perchance I may think myself so much better than I am, as that they who are about me, and see my state, may have caused it to toll for me, and I know not that.

The church is Catholic, universal, so are all her actions; all that she does belongs to all.

When she baptizes a child, that action concerns me; for that child is thereby connected to that body which is my head too, and ingrafted into that body whereof I am a member.

And when she buries a man, that action concerns me: all mankind is of one author, and is one volume; when one man dies, one chapter is not torn out of the book, but translated into a better language; and every chapter must be so translated; God employs several translators; some pieces are translated by age, some by sickness, some by war, some by justice; but God's hand is in every translation, and his hand shall bind up all our scattered leaves again for that library where every book shall lie open to one another.

As therefore the bell that rings to a sermon calls not upon the preacher only, but upon the congregation to come, so this bell calls us all; but how much more me, who am brought so near the door by this sickness.

There was a contention as far as a suit (in which both piety and dignity, religion and estimation, were mingled), which of the religious orders should ring to prayers first in the morning; and it was determined, that they should ring first that rose earliest.

If we understand aright the dignity of this bell that tolls for our evening prayer, we would be glad to make it ours by rising early, in that application, that it might be ours as well as his, whose indeed it is.

The bell doth toll for him that thinks it doth; and though it intermit again, yet from that minute that this occasion wrought upon him, he is united to God.

Who casts not up his eye to the sun when it rises? But who takes off his eye from a comet when that breaks out? Who bends not his ear to any bell which upon any occasion rings? But who can remove it from that bell which is passing a piece of himself out of this world? No man is an island, entire of itself; every man is a piece of the continent, a part of the main.

If a clod be washed away by the sea, Europe is the less, as well as if a promontory were, as well as if a manor of thy friend's or of thine own were: any man's death diminishes me, because I am involved in mankind, and therefore never send to know for whom the bell tolls; it tolls for thee. Neither can we call this a begging of misery, or a borrowing of misery, as though we were not miserable enough of ourselves, but must fetch in more from the next house, in taking upon us the misery of our neighbours.

Truly it were an excusable covetousness if we did, for affliction is a treasure, and scarce any man hath enough of it.

No man hath affliction enough that is not matured and ripened by it, and made fit for God by that affliction.

If a man carry treasure in bullion, or in a wedge of gold, and have none coined into current money, his treasure will not defray him as he travels.

Tribulation is treasure in the nature of it, but it is not current money in the use of it, except we get nearer and nearer our home, heaven, by it.

Another man may be sick too, and sick to death, and this affliction may lie in his bowels, as gold in a mine, and be of no use to him; but this bell, that tells me of his affliction, digs out and applies that gold to me: if by this consideration of another's danger I take mine own into contemplation, and so secure myself, by making my recourse to my God, who is our only security.

Besides teaching our students about literature and poetry, we also teach them about community. This essay certainly reflects the 17th century and the writer's personal relationship with his church and his God. I am taking what I want from it, what applies to my situation in the 21st century, ideas that I think have a universal ring. Whatever happens to any one of affects all of us, if not directly then certainly shortly thereafter. No man is an island, entire unto itself. Teenagers may act as though they are not a part of the main, but it is our job as adults to remind them that they are. They know it, but from time to time they need to be reminded. We all need to listen when the bell tolls.

THE DEAN DECADE

I want to put my tenure as Dean in the context of the national times. Despite sometimes feeling that we live in a small village or in a world of our own, we are connected to the outside world. With our international population and with many well-read students and parents, we cannot, even if wanted to, divorce ourselves from the larger world.

During my tenure as Dean there have been some defining events in the United States: election of Clinton/Gore (1992); Waco and the World Trade Center (1993); OJ Simpson (1994); the Oklahoma City bombing (1995); Monica Lewinsky (1995-1999); Olympics in Atlanta and the arrest of the Unabomber (1996); the death of Princess Diana (1997); the impeachment and trial of the President of the United States (1998-99); Columbine (1999); the Presidential election and the chads (2000); and September 11 (2001). Certainly two of the last three had more direct impact on life at the school, but every year had its defining moments both nationally and locally in our village.

As many pundits and leaders have discussed, the danger is that fear itself will overtake us. Did life change dramatically for us, particularly after 9/11, and will we be permanently looking over our shoulders rather than focusing on what is ahead? Will we be constricted by our fears from acting as we should?

Not often have I been involved directly with the local police department in dealing with violence or potential violence. The image of metal detectors at our doors, of armed officers roaming the campus, of ID checks all over the school: these not only would be foreign to us, they would be anathema. At worst is that these restrictions will eventually happen. At some point we may lose a life on campus to violence. Such an exceptional act should not cause us to alter our fundamental commitments as to how we practice what we practice. But I confess that I think about loss of life on campus from time to time.

Suicide is violent as well, and while we have not had a suicide in my tenure as Dean, the school has had two in my 33 years as a teacher. I had direct experience with one. A suicide demands that we look at what we are doing as an institution, but more often it causes us to reflect on the particular individual and reassess what we did or did not do for that particular person. We do not see suicide as a pervasive concern at the forefront of our daily lives. But that concern lurks beneath the surface, closer during certain times of the year that are becoming increasingly, though not infallibly, predictable. Spring, for instance, rather than winter has higher rates of suicide, and yet we think of spring as blooming and optimistic and winter as dreary and depressing.

Nevertheless, when we have identified an individual we feel is at risk—and this always involves the professional assessment by trained evaluators—we intervene directly. I know we have prevented suicides and serious drug/alcohol related tragedies by our actions. On rare occasions we have only postponed them because the issues were not resolved inside the individuals.

Anti-social violence has been rare at my school. Having a strong statement about our concern for each other as well as for the community as a whole has set a tone from the first day of a student's involvement. We have evolved from having pre-season athletes arriving in the fall before other students, as the responsibility only of the athletic department or of an individual coach, to having these students be part of the formal school matriculation. On the evening of the first day of pre-season athlete arrivals, we have had a Dean's meeting with the students to ensure that they know that school rules apply. Meeting the Dean officially carries more weight than the formal letter in the summer or the receipt of the Student Handbook with all its details. Contact with people who have personalities as well as titles carries far more weight than written introductions. Students know from that first day—information is then repeated for international students when they first arrive for an orientation, for new boarding students, and for all the students when they finally have come to school—that what we say in our Handbook, what we say in our philosophical statements, what we say personally, is what will be the expected behavior for all of us. When there are transgressions, by design or by mistake, there will be consequences. Virtually the only exception to our practice of helping kids grow through their errors is when there is violence or the threat of it.

I have seen a gun once in the possession of a student (and my assistant was given one by a teacher who had confiscated a target pistol from another student). The student I confronted did not have the gun on his person, but he did have it in his room. It was not there long because he showed it to at least one other student who eventually had that information passed to me. I learned specifically where it was, confirmed it, and confronted the student. He willingly gave it up.

Several circumstances contributed to his being expelled from school, but there was thoughtful assessment of the boy and the circumstances. He decided not to withdraw from school prior to discipline; he wanted to appeal through the Discipline Committee. The Committee felt he could not remain. At least three important reasons contributed to their recommendation. One was that the boy had been involved in an event two years earlier where he had cut his roommate with a broken cup. The roommate had been lacerated badly enough that the police and ambulance were called, and he had extensive stitching and then plastic surgery. There were two accounts to what had happened, each with truth in them, and both boys remained at the school under strict guidelines. Neither boy nor the respective set of parents were fully satisfied; how could they be after an incident that would leave permanent scars, at least one of which was physical?

A second circumstance involved marijuana; the boy had been on Probation for possession and use. There was ongoing concern as well, but nothing further had been proven.

Finally, the boy had fired the gun in his dorm room. He had wanted to test it out so he successfully muffled the sound and had put a bullet hole in a target that was hidden from view to someone simply being in the room. He had told other students he had done this and admitted it to the Discipline Committee. That decision—to fire the gun with ammunition—suggested a lack of judgment inconsistent with our school expectations.

Despite ongoing counseling, despite parents who were supportive and actively involved, despite his sincere appeal to the Discipline Committee, the Committee felt—representing the entire community—that he could not be allowed to continue at the school. The firing of the gun in the dorm room left the Committee shaken about this individual's ability to make the right decision in this community. He could not stay.

In the larger context, the ability of this student to purchase a gun through a mail order sale, have it delivered to his home, from where he then brought it to school, and to have it unregistered—unknown to anyone else, including his parents who had a credit card bill from a sporting goods supply store—worries me still. And this was pre-Columbine.

Earlier in the 2001-2002 school year in a Massachusetts public school in New Bedford, another potential Columbine-like massacre may have been prevented because a student was fearful enough that she told a teacher about what was planned. That led to an investigation, arrests, and probably a prevention of another horrific event.

In both the New Bedford case and mine, of which mine had little relevance to what happened at Columbine, students themselves took the initiative to prevent something they were afraid might happen. Somehow these reporting students had felt they had to act rather than not act. They did not feel they had to act directly, but they did feel they had to tell someone who would act. In my school, there was a great deal of relief when this student finally left the school, although no student publicly expressed such a sentiment. Privately, a number said so to others and me. In New Bedford, I can only imagine the relief that many people must have felt.

All it takes for evil to succeed is for good people to do nothing;

a small sentence I heard somewhere and I like to repeat from time to time. And sometimes it is not evil that will happen; it might just be some unfortunate or tragic accident.

I have the opportunity virtually every day to act or not act, which of course in itself is an act. While I have the capacity to beat myself up with guilt, I am learning not to be paralyzed by it. Nevertheless, I reflect on events that happened that I might have prevented.

One night when I was on duty the school play was being performed at the theater. I wandered over prior to the performance and encountered a car with several of our commuting students. Some of them I knew were troubled kids and I had a suspicion that they had been drinking. They did not want to get out of the car, were not eager to talk, and I suggested they go home. I decided to stop in my office and call the parents of one of the students in the car, someone I had had conversation with before. I cannot remember whether his daughter was the driver of the car, but I suggested that if they showed up at his house that he might want to make inquiries and perhaps keep them home for the remainder of the evening.

Early the next morning I had a call in my office from the father. His daughter had been in a serious car accident on the way home, and she was badly injured. Rather than berating me for not doing something, which could have been a logical reaction, he simply told me that my intuition about trouble was right and that he had appreciated the call the night before.

She suffered through several operations, plastic surgery and perhaps even therapy for her trauma. Fortunately, she was eventually able to move on.

The story is not about her but about me. Would that I had forced them out of the car, called the parents or the police, and held them from their self-destructive behavior. Anyone having dealt with the social dynamics of villages and especially ones replete with teenagers would see my decision as a problematic response. I might not have succeeded in getting them out of the car, would have had an unpleasant confrontation with a win/lose agenda at that time, and would have jeopardized whatever cachet I might have had with the student body as a whole. The predictability of the disaster that followed was not apparent. I had a difficult choice, and the outcome for the victims of the car crash was not what they wanted. But I can also spin out other scenarios with other disastrous outcomes from that incident. I had to make a judgment, and perhaps in the long run it was indeed the right one. Perhaps that is rationalization, perhaps just weighing other "what ifs." I cannot be in the business of saving all teenagers from either themselves or from others. I can only hope that I am trying to be "good enough."

After Columbine, we all have a concern for what might happen. We are less tolerant of potential anti-social behavior as well as the actual anti-social behavior. One answer would be for all students to have less opportunity to appear different or to act differently. I think that was called Brave New World.

I would prefer that the adults in the community be more involved, more aware. When the alienated and disaffected show the signs that they are having problems, intervention for the individual will prove to be excellent preventive medicine. However, intervention will have a successful outcome if the student has a connection with some adult. When adults force themselves into a student's life it needs to be because that is the last resort. Force might mean that intervention is too late, but it is certainly better than continuing to ignore the problem. And requiring the student to have a relationship with an adult, unlike simply encouraging the student, may start a healthy relationship.

In our school we have three methods of opening a formal relationship between a student and a therapist. The first is voluntary; the student simply seeks out our school psychologist and enters into a confidential relationship. Anyone can encourage this beginning—the student, friends, some adult—but it would only be a suggestion or perhaps even a plea. Peers have been successful in attempts to initiate conversations because as a community we have encouraged it and because the students have a concern for their friends. Usually it is self-destructive behavior that motivates students to counsel their friends: eating disorders, self-mutilation (cutting oneself has been on the rise recently), and depressing conversation.

The second method is for an adult to contract with the student to see the psychologist with the stipulation that the fact that a meeting occurred be reported to the adult. I have often done with this with students who I think are struggling with issues. With me there is always the underlying sense that a formal disciplinary response is looming, and certainly from a student's perspective a discussion with the psychologist might be better than a discussion with parents!

The third is the more formal interventionist approach, not often used, where an administrator in the school mandates the student to have a formal evaluation. A report is submitted to the administrator mandating the meeting. This intervention follows a behavior that is of concern to an administrator, usually someone in the Dean's Office. Still, the student has a choice; perhaps the less attractive option is to leave the school. That leaving the school would be less attractive suggests a comfort level that reflects a generally healthy environment.

We—as all schools—have some terrific kids. Some might even be talented, beyond the normal expectation of doing a good job in class, or on the athletic field, or in extra-curricular activities. Some become student leaders—as proctors, as student council members, as Discipline Committee members. Some go on to outstanding colleges as scholars, some to Division I athletic programs, some to art programs where productions and performances get special notice. Yet by terrific, I mean something different. I mean those kids who are willing to act on behalf of other kids, who are willing to take steps to either solve a problem or prevent a problem. Those kinds of kids exist in all schools; sometimes, though, they slip by the adults or the "system".

I am impressed—proud—when students are able to get a peer to talk with an adult who can help them. It means that the student has a solid reputation with the peer, and that both students have confidence in someone in the adult community to help them resolve a problem.

A junior girl, bright, athletic, artistically talented, was having difficulty coping with her own expectations—as well as those of her parents' hopes and dreams—and manifested this struggle with an eating disorder. I never really knew the exact disorder, but it was probably bulimia, the act of eating and then throwing up later. The desire to become thin—or thinner—conflicts with another concern; people may notice her not eating properly in the dining commons. So she ate normally and then threw up later, hoping perhaps people would not notice her behavior. They did. Because she had many good friends they persuaded her to go to the Health Service and deal with problem. I think there was a threat that if the girl did not go herself, her friends would report her and have it be a more formal, and thereby more public, act. We might argue about the word "threat," which sounds too strong and negative, but teenagers know full well how to motivate their peers to act. Going to an adult, even a professional like a school psychologist or Dean, is not subtle pressure to a teenager. That becomes the alternative to having the person go herself. She went.

My knowledge of this event came mostly from reading clues that I would hear or see, and although I wanted to make sure the situation was in someone's control I did not want the Dean to be involved as Dean. I have learned to monitor from enough distance that I will not stick my nose where it does not belong and hinder what good therapy may result. Nevertheless, I could not resist making sure the girl was doing ok, even making a point to be just a little bit more friendly than normal. She knew that I knew, knew that I was concerned and cared, knew that I did not intend to intrude, even though I felt I almost blew it, which I told her. One result was a box of goodies and a beautiful card at Christmas, simply saying thanks. I am sure that she was at least as generous to her peer friends who did more than I to get her to seek help. I think this incident was evidence of the culture that we have developed that allows such action to happen.

Another student leader came to me with concern about her friend who was having terrible guilt about being with another student who earlier in the year had been drinking and was caught at a school dance. The drinker had been caught and punished in the usual fashion, but the friend had had one drink and had been with the drinker. She, however, had not been determined to have had any behavior that warranted disciplinary action. She had escaped detection. However, she had not escaped her own sense of guilt. Weeks later she was still upset about how she had been guilty of being "in the presence of" and in the fact of drinking. She was also fearful that she would be discovered and would be punished.

The girl who came to me asked if her friend were indeed in danger of penalty because she was concerned about her friend's guilt-racked behavior, which included emotional fragility, lack of sleep, and inability to eat. I assured her that the case was closed, but I would be happy to talk to her friend directly as a kind of adviser rather than as Dean.

The two of them came to my office, and it was clear that the girl was having great difficulty dealing with her own sense of guilt. She finally agreed after we talked more than once that she would see the school psychologist, and that she would agree that I had knowledge that that meeting had taken place. History suggests we had intervened successfully. Both of the girls rank as terrific teenagers, and they were willing to work together as well as with appropriate adults. Terrific kids are not without their fears and difficulties; we cannot elevate any to icons, despite our desire to do that from time to time.

The third type of intervention is the result of a more difficult situation. I have been involved in several. They are not pleasant, they are not comfortable, and sometimes they are frightening. My own experiences have not involved school-wide concerns; they were not potential Columbines, but there was violence and the threat of it.

Perhaps all violence means there should have been psychological and therapeutic involvement prior to the incident, even in a situation of "flight or fight." The news provides enough examples to make my stories mild. Recently, a father was convicted of 2nd degree manslaughter after he beat a man to death at a hockey rink by banging the man's head on the floor repeatedly. He was angry at the way the man, a youth team coach, had been allowing and perhaps encouraging violent play to go on during practice. An argument ensued, words led to actions. A father died.

The jury determined that the man had indeed been attacked and was threatened, but the victim weighed 100 pounds less than the man who beat him and the beating went on much longer than a simple self-defense. At least that was the conclusion of the jury, who convicted the man to perhaps 20 years in prison. His child and the victim's own three children had witnessed the beating, certainly adding to the emotion of the situation.

Both of the fathers had histories of violence so reconstruction of the incident with all the background information makes the case even more shocking in the context of lives that had complex and predictable tendencies.

We finally told a student and his family that he could not return after several incidents over the course of several years. That he was at our school for 2 ½ years at all attests, I hope, to our optimism about what can happen to bright and talented kids if they can get the help and direction they need to overcome difficulties that are not of their own making. Or it could mean we were naïve, indecisive, and weak. Perhaps he should not have been admitted in the first place; there were concerns from a psychologist who had been involved with him prior to his matriculation. He had run away from home and been returned by state officials, been under the care of DSS (Department of Social Services, which means the state had taken control of his life because the family was unable to), and exhibited tendencies towards oppositional disorder; he did not like authority. Yet he was very bright.

In his first year he had gotten into fights in the dorm, threatened other students, made inappropriate comments; generally, people thought he was disturbed. He was interviewed at our office and we sent him to Health Services for a psychological evaluation. His parents arrived, and when they went to see him at Health Services he became furious, yelling at his parents, telling us (both the Assistant Head and myself were involved at this point), that we had no right to involve his parents. He barricaded himself in a room at the Health Services, and we finally called the police. His mother did not speak English, his father seemed to have little control over the boy.

I think we were seeing signs of a disturbed boy.

Yes, we did know this.

Given the option of going home or Sectioned 12 (taken to the psychiatric wing at the hospital), he calmed down and agreed to go with his parents.

We sent him home for a time, changed his dorm when he returned and placed him near a teacher who had made a good connection with him. He was in therapy and refocused on what he had to do. We were hopeful.

The remainder of the year and the next year went better than what we might have hoped for. Part of the problem was that he was better off with us than he was at home. He even went so far as to find another family that he had become close to, and they were in the process of taking full custody. Our guarded optimism about both the particular situation and teenagers in general caused us to push on through clearly troubled waters; but we also were not sure what the alternatives were.

While we are not a therapeutic institution in the sense of having the facilities, the staff, or the psychological preparation to deal with deeply troubled kids, we do work frequently with therapists to try to have a good school work for kids who are not necessarily fully prepared to meet the obligations and expectations we impose. Sometimes we are not successful.

In the middle of his third year the boy finally lost control of himself, and one night he barricaded himself into his room, threatened violence, threatened to leave the dorm late at night after check-in, and I had to call Emergency Service at the local hospital to send over a counselor to help us get through to him. After lengthy negotiation, the boy finally emerged and went to a hospital, where he remained for an extended period.

We had to separate him from the school because he clearly could not function in this environment. He had psychological problems that needed to be addressed in a more comprehensive manner. Although relieved, we were also saddened. We had utilized all the resources we had: a good teacher, counseling services, frequent communication with guardian and parents. We did not have all the information we should have had before we admitted the boy 2 ½ years earlier, and perhaps we should not have admitted him if we knew what we learned later. Yet we were hopeful.

Did we fail? One of my pet philosophies has been: the sin is not trying and failing, but failing to try. We certainly would have saved ourselves hours of work and anxiety, but the story is perhaps not yet over. Perhaps we will never know what happened to this individual, and perhaps we made an impact that has not yet been revealed.

Another incident, a little more chilling to me personally, had more to do with a mother than with her son. He finally went to a Discipline Committee hearing one Wednesday afternoon and was expelled after a series of incidents. His mother was lingering in the hallway and after she heard the verdict she accosted me. "Who are you?" she wanted to know. We had talked on the phone several times but had not had the pleasure of a meeting. When I told her who I was she, loudly, proclaimed:" Well, you can drop dead. And the last person I said that to is six feet under!" A student in the hallway heard it and the switchboard operator heard it. They were shaken. Fortunately, the woman left the building. I called my friend at the police station to record the event. I also had the two witnesses give me statements to corroborate the prediction. I did not hear from her again, and I am hopeful I can finish this account before my appointed time.

There was no doubt her son was a problem, and there was no doubt she had one herself. That evening I learned even more about what had happened that caused her son to finally earn his just desserts, and she was more clearly implicated in the situation than I had realized. In the long run it probably helped our relationship with the local constabulary as well, because they had made an error that I was disappointed with.

There is an element to this tale that belongs in the section on Politics so I will return to this particular saga in another context.

The student had accumulated an exemplary record of disciplinary violations. He had arrived in September after a late admittance by the Admissions Office (see Politics) as a boarding student. We did not have room in the Day category, nor would he have qualified in comparison with other candidates to fill the limited number of spots we had available. Promptly he was in jeopardy because he was found with three girls in his room one afternoon. He—and his parents—claimed ignorance of the rule, that the girls went up the stairs to his room voluntarily and uninvited, and that the rule should not apply anyway because it was an event unworthy of such a response. The Discipline Committee felt otherwise. He was placed on Probation.

Two months later a room search after he returned from a weekend revealed drug paraphernalia in his roommate's possession. He claimed ignorance of the material, and despite grounds for Separation the school allowed him to continue because the circumstances were fuzzy enough to leave room for doubt, albeit very little room.

By April he had accumulated 8 Units, one shy of another Probation, and in fact had persuaded teachers on at least 2 occasions not to give him a 9th so that he would not once again have to go before the Discipline Committee.

Then he was accused of behavior over the weekend that put him in serious jeopardy and which called for a Discipline Committee hearing. He had been involved with some hazing activity in the dorm (all supposed good fun by the peer group!), which included some abuse and destruction of personal property of another student. The dorm parents were totally exasperated with this student. On Monday his parents took him home because there was a threat of a big snowstorm; this also avoided the Discipline Committee for that afternoon. We rescheduled for Wednesday.

As in a number of cases I have worked with, the students unwittingly provided hard evidence of their own activities: pictures. We had photographs the students had taken of themselves horsing around during this alleged hazing and destruction. There was a picture of a freshman kneeling on all fours with a noose around his neck. He was smiling. We were not. There was a picture of the student in question holding scissors about to cut something. In addition, the student had written an account of the activities that was absolutely contrary to what was true as evidenced by the pictures and statements from other students. There was little debate over the outcome of the committee's deliberations. Shortly thereafter came the Drop Dead statement.

One of the students on the Discipline Committee later revealed that he knew something additional that was not part of the deliberation. There had been rumor of some alcohol purchase the previous Friday evening, but there was no evidence beyond the rumor stage. The student let me know—after I was to Drop Dead— that in fact this student had been arrested the previous Friday evening for attempting to purchase alcohol with a false ID. Because he was 17 he was charged; another boy with him, who was younger, was not charged and was released. Apparently the older boy called his parents, who arrived at the police station and berated the police for doing what they did. Sadly, I was not a fly on the wall for that conversation. The parents took him, called the school to say that they had suddenly taken him home because he was stressed, and that they wanted to give him some time to rest and relieve the stress caused by all the pressures of school.

Inexplicably, the police did not inform us. These were two boarding students, under our jurisdiction. I confirmed that the incident indeed had taken place, but I did not get a satisfactory explanation of why we were never informed. This, too, probably deserves a space in Politics, but I can only speculate. Allegedly, the family lived next door to the Chief of Police in their town, but whether that made any difference I don't know.

Since the above-related incident, though not necessarily related to any cause and effect, our relations with the local police—always quite good—became even better. Part of the reason is that they know that the school handles infractions like marijuana possession, alcohol possession, and other misdemeanor offenses more expeditiously and more firmly than they do. They have more serious crime to work on, and they are happy to work with us. Sometimes they can use our help, and often we can use theirs. Again, prevention and interdiction before more serious offenses happen is in everyone's best interests.

Kids grow up, and most of them do not need added legal baggage to what they are already carrying. There are a few successful adults in our midst—leaders in our community, parents, teachers—who had some scrapes with the police as teenagers. I am not arguing that serious violent crime be erased from juvenile records, but there is wisdom in clearing the record of much of what juveniles do. If they repeat criminal offenses as adults, the consequences are already more severe. The teachable moment with the police during the teenage years has a lasting effect for most students.

I have been to the police station on occasion. I think there is a former student who still owes me $25 for bail that I had to provide. And he was not even a boarding student. The old police station was not comfortable or very attractive in the interior. The new one is not meant to be comfortable for those locked up, but it is certainly a more professional facility. When I had to bail out this particular student, he was handcuffed to what I recall was a pipe in an interview room; but it may have been something else. It was not a pleasant scene for either the student or myself. He had a forlorn look as he sat there, sheepishly looking at me as I waited for the process to have him released completed. He had been in trouble before so he knew he was about to go home that afternoon, perhaps permanently severing his ties with the school. He had been arrested smoking marijuana in town somewhere, and he told them he was a student at my school. The police had to call me at my home.

Just another wise-ass kid, another statistic in our ongoing war with drugs and juvenile crime, another small bite on our societal butt that we wish would just go away. And I was called away from my pregnant wife at the end of another typical day at school. He had already been in trouble so we were faced with the likelihood that he would be Dismissed. But of course, there were "circumstances" so we considered options. He wrote to us.

I am writing In order to respond to the waiver that was recently sent to me.

First and foremost I would like to thank [the adults at the school] for their openness and guidance through what has been a difficult time. You have all been very honest and up front with me, and I appreciate the chance to express my thoughts about the situation so far.

I have followed up on your concern about my substance abuse problem, and had a complete assessment at the . . . Hospital. . . . The assessment resulted in a recommendation that I receive outpatient treatment for my problem; they felt that an inpatient program was not what I needed. I have started counseling. . . . I have given my counselor permission to communicate with [the school] about my situation. [The counselor] has tried to help me to determine when my problem started and what seemed to lead up to it. It was a surprise to me to discover that my use of drugs seems to be related in time to the crisis that our family went through three years ago when my mother's cancer was discovered. With [the counselor] I discovered the sadness, fear, and anger that surrounds this experience, which I seem to have avoided. I was very shocked. I had almost totally forgotten that part of my life. I remember how terrified I was and realize that I still am. I have discovered that it put me over the edge. I thought I was going to lose my mother. I didn't exactly know what Cancer was, I didn't need to, the word terrified me when my mom first said it at the dinner table. I thought I was going to lose my mother. I felt helpless as anyone would, when the strongest people in their life seem so vulnerable. I started using pot soon after. After my mother's surgery things seemed to return to normal for me, or so I thought. These past few days I have realized In talking to [the counselor] that the long period of radiation and chemotherapy went on for almost two years. I think that these events have harmed my sense of judgment, reality, emotion, and responsibility. Although I have been calm and collected in our meetings, I am being torn up inside. The anger and sadness that I feel are for myself. I had turned to pot as a way to avoid my feelings. I am becoming more and more aware of what has happened to my life, and the mistakes that I have made, and the need for me to take full responsibility for them.

This crisis has brought me to my senses, and I realize how much I need [school]. Not just because of my six years of attendance but because I need to make amends. I want so badly to stand up on the stage this June, and get my diploma drug-free. This is by far the most distraught I have ever been. It feels as if my whole life has bottomed out. Everything in the past and future stands atop my head, not to mention the present situation, and I would like to propose an alternate form of the waiver that recognizes the need for [the school's] disciplinary system to be upheld, and yet allows me to continue to participate in the [school] community with my class.

I realize that without the two probations this year on my record, I would probably have received a week's suspension, along with other things such as a drug-free contract and probation. I know that I deserve something more of a punishment than that, yet I hope for less than the separation that is proposed in the waiver, I Would like to suggest that in addition to probation and a "no-use" contract, I receive at least 2 Weeks suspension, that I also be allowed to do community service on the weekends until final exams, that I participate In the peer educator Program, and that I come back to an assembly next year to speak to the students about my experience.

I would also like to suggest that I be allowed to return to my classes for the duration of the school year, after my suspension period, and would promise to leave the campus at 5.30 each day, or after my last commitment, and that I would not drive to campus for classes at all. I would also drop my captainship of the Lacrosse team.

This experience has been a painful one, but I have a new understanding of what has been happening in my life, and I will continue on this healthier path regardless of how things turn out in the short run. Nevertheless, I hope that you feel that my proposal is reasonable. I need to prove to the school, my parents, and myself that I can get my life together. I want to succeed at [the school], but first I need you to help me in this one last way.

Thank you for your consideration.

I knew much of this student's background already, but it was not appropriate for us to debate it in public. For me, he was not "Just another wise-ass kid, another statistic in our ongoing war with drugs and juvenile crime, another small bite on our societal butt that we wish would just go away." He did go away for the rest of the semester, which was appropriate considering his record, but he did attend the graduation ceremony and received his diploma in August.

I do not know what the next several chapters in his life have been; I hope they turn out well.

POWER AND AUTHORITY

Working with the police complements my work as Dean, but I remind myself that there is a danger in getting caught up with the sense of power or in the name-dropping associated with conversations. I am not comfortable with the sense of power, though I use it, but I am comfortable with the sense of authority.

Authority is another of those exciting words. It connotes power, and from the students' perspective it is almost incumbent upon them to test the authority, even oppose it. Yet the word is often used with contempt, and like discipline it is misunderstood.

The root of the word comes from the same source as that of author. People (even students!), are not uncomfortable being the author of a work, the creator, instigator or initiator; unless, of course, the result causes some kind of harm, at which point there is sometimes a scramble to distance oneself from the authorship.

But students often perceive authority as distant from authorship. The Dean did not create the school or its rules; the Dean only enforces the rules. So the Dean (or anyone with power: Headmaster, dorm parent, teacher) does not carry the weight of authorship. He is only a tool of the system from that perspective.

In any community there is an authority; even the anarchist obeys himself. How that authority is exercised is more the point rather than the existence of authority per se.

The two other spin-offs from the word are authoritarian and authoritative. These represent the more applicable sense of the word—authority—and the concept behind it.

An authoritarian is one who insists on obedience, in an unquestioned manner. Power flows in one direction, obedience the other. The authoritarian brooks no question of the origin of that power. It simply exists, and he has it. Sometimes we can refer to those who slavishly obey or bow to the authoritarian as also authoritarian. There is a convenient symmetry, an either/or. The person who rose to the top usually has had little countenance with compromise, with negotiation, with tolerance. Certainly the authoritarian style is efficient. When the authoritarian is right, the community functions smoothly. However, almost by definition the authoritarian cannot be wrong, and thus if the community is not running smoothly the problem cannot be with the decision. The problem must be with the followers.

Schools, at least in the United States, did not grow from an authoritarian decision. The United States itself did not grow from an authoritarian seed, although there were indeed plenty of examples of those seeds scattered in the forest primeval of the colonial days. They simply did not flourish in the environment. They surface from time to time, but they are somewhat like a lemon tree. The fruit usually must mix with something else to be palatable.

The Dean of Discipline (much more appropriately of Students) cannot be successful as an authoritarian. And that is a challenge for many. It is like the lemon standing alone. The successful Dean (or authority person), cannot function without exercising power. The label "permissive" is often used to discredit the style that is not decisive.

In the middle ground is "authoritative." The sense of that term reflects willingness to use legitimate power for appropriate ends. It is more thoughtful than decisive, more inclusive than arbitrary, more flexible than rigid.

Because I am not authoritarian by nature, I have more experiences with "permissive" actions that have put me on the hot seat than with authoritarian actions. I also have some examples of authoritative actions. But for the most part I do not even think in those terms, except as I am referring to other people!

Most often authoritarian and permissive acts for me have been opposite sides of the same coin. I either allowed a student to do something contrary to what someone else wanted or I did not. The perspective determines the label, and that to a large degree exempts me from the authoritarian tag.

A student's parents called me one spring to ask if their son could miss a track meet to attend a wrestling tournament. On the surface the answer was easy enough. He had an obligation to the school's track team. That came first. But the parents persuaded me that because this particular boy was struggling with several issues, he would be better served, and in the long run the school would be better served, if he could attend this tournament. It was only a junior varsity wrestling tournament, and he clearly was not committed to the track team. Nevertheless, his absence from the track meet would put the coach in a bind trying to fill his spot.

Naturally, I was not high on the honored list in the athletic department for allowing the student to attend the wrestling meet.

The boy finished the spring and decided not to return to school the following year. He was unhappy, had had difficulty with alcohol, and was clearly a risk for us and to himself. What if . . . ? Maybe he would have left school before the end of the year, maybe he would have had another unhappy incident with alcohol, maybe . . . . In hindsight, I am still comfortable with the decision I made. The boy and his family left the school on comfortable terms, the track team did not fall apart, and I was still the Dean the next year. We moved on.

Was it permissive to have given in to the parents' request? It was not authoritarian because I was not completely comfortable with the choice that I had made. But someone was going to be unhappy with my decision. And I was the authority.

Nevertheless, we did make some rule changes so that there would be school consequences for such an absence. There can always be consequences by the coach ("you won't play in the next game"), but now we give the student at least a school enforced unexcused absence as a consequence for the choice that had to be made. It sounds so logical in hindsight. There will no doubt be a situation when again there will have to be some arbitrary decision by the Dean that makes at least someone unhappy, but there is no doubt more comfort now in the "system" than there was.

One systemic change I feel I can take significant credit for was the hours for evening study in the dorms. Most schools like ours operated on a timetable where students had to be in the dorm from 7:30-9:30 for at least quiet time, unless they had exceptions, (seniors on Honors, play rehearsal, proctor privilege, etc.). Then there was a half hour when students could be outside the dorm until they had to check in for the night at 10 PM.

We changed that to study hall from 8-10 with no out-of-dorm activity afterwards. Underclass students had to be in their own rooms at 10:30 and seniors at 11:00. There was great angst as we discussed this within the faculty and within the Student Council. The adjustment would be too hard, the loss of privilege too great, the opportunity to blow off steam would be lost, etc.

My argument, eventually supported by the majority within our dorm heads' group, pointed to the downsides of the half hour out of the dorm: opportunity to sneak a cigarette (we are a tobacco-free campus), opportunity to meet one's significant other or friends in general (which meant preparation well before the 9:30 study hall ended), the practice of stocking up on such useful pre-bedtime items like caffeine drinks and junk food. Behind one group of dormitories was an area in the woods with a small river running through it. It also bordered on private property that was not the school's. It was a well-used spot for a variety of activities: sun-bathing in the warm weather, swimming, smoking, drinking. All of those activities made dorm life for the faculty, as well as for many of the students, far too hectic from 9:30-10:30 and then later in the night. Many years of student activities had given that area the reputation of being a sanctuary from adult eyes. It has taken us as a school a few years to change that attitude, but for the moment it is understood as a place where a student would risk serious consequences. Removing the area as a sanctuary after dark, and certainly as a secure place from 9:30-10:00, would represent a positive change for those in authority.

We braced ourselves for fallout, and it never came. Nor has anyone looked back or even faintly suggested we return to the previous system. Everyone has benefited, and even students who lived under both systems recognized the improvement in the quality of life in the dorm. It was calmer, more congenial, more communal. The change had been the right one.

Even with this example, I am not sure that authoritative is the right word. Persuasive, rational, sound—all might better serve the interpretation of the decision.

Perhaps my style is better revealed in the issue of hats. Everyone in our school knows wearing hats in certain indoor areas is illegal. We can penalize students for wearing them, giving what is called a Unit for a dress code violation. Some people automatically give a Unit, although not many of the adult population want to take that action in a more public or communal place. In their own classroom, teachers are much more comfortable wielding authority. More are apt to ignore the situation completely, unless they specifically know the student. There are even occasional instances where a teacher may choose to ignore the violation entirely because the rule seems petty to that individual. That is more a Dean of Faculty or Headmaster issue, nevertheless one that needs to be addressed at some point. It's just not usually my area; some would want me to take it on, but I'll defer to a higher power.

My own style is to let the student know he or she is breaking the rule, and most often the student has genuinely forgotten to take the hat off. It is no surprise to me that simple eye contact from even 50 feet away gets the job done, and with no complaint. But there are exceptions, and students know full well when they deserve a Unit.

However, lest anyone think I am a kingly persona who acts as a magnet in a room, I have had to work hard to appear authoritative. I am basically shy, often diffident, not prone to inserting myself into situations. I have come to accept my responsibility, even stewardship, within my community or village.

Stewardship is another of those words that I enjoy. It is also one of those words that will generate disbelief and snide abuse by a majority of the population. It seems pompous, paternalistic, and unnecessary. So I like it.

In the constant struggle between the individual and the community, the guardians of the community as a whole must at times sacrifice their own individuality to an even greater extent than the vast majority of the populace. They have a greater responsibility to the community, both for the present and the future.

I do see myself as a steward. I am not a visionary, someone with a future goal that I want to work towards. I think my community is on an appropriate path, heading in the right direction, flawed as any community is because it is made up of human beings. The steward's job is to act as a guide, a supporter, a resource, a member of the community.

One of the dangers of the leader is that he may have an eye only on what is in front. An image I have seen in inspirational quips is that of the herd, with the notation that every member has the same view except for the one in front. The leader needs to have people to minister to those in the rest of the community while the leader leads. These are the stewards. Both the leader and the stewards need to practice stewardship, and hopefully they will encourage new stewards to rise to that role. If the leader or his stewards treat the community as a herd, the community will fail.

The Dean of Stewardship. It won't play well as a title, and neither does Dean of Discipline or Dean of Dress. Titles and trappings are not as important as substance.

Leader is another useful term to dissect, although leadership is more important to the one who leads. Here again my experience as a teacher of the Hitler and Nazi Germany course has been useful. The German word for leader was fuhrer. Hitler capitalized it and applied it to himself, not only as a title but also in a philosophical sense. He was the embodiment of everything his movement stood for, the incarnation of the true prophet and the leader of a new German nation. By definition, what he said was true; by implication, any contradiction of what he said was false and even treasonous. He was infallible.

Infallibility is not appropriate for human beings. It has short-term advantages when the actions are right, but right is a judgmental term best applied after the fact, sometimes long after the fact. Leadership style in the context of our American history and its values has included advice from differing perspectives and then a willingness to act and take the consequences later. In the parlor game style of ranking Presidents by historians or even average citizens, those who exercised this kind of leadership earn the highest praise: Lincoln, FDR, Washington. Truman's rank has been rising as we reassess Presidents from time to time, and he will certainly be remembered for his desktop motto: the buck stops here. The good leader has to know when to make decisions, and even when not to make them.

The buck does not stop on my desk, at least for the biggest decisions concerning students in a school. There is always the possibility of an appeal to one of my bosses, but it certainly is easier on my bosses if the decisions I make are the ones that they also agree with. It is also helpful to have a systemic approach to the knotty problems of accumulated minor troubles. Our Discipline Committee gives the community an opportunity to participate in determining the outcome for a given student. It is also a way to have another input prior to a decision, delaying an important decision from the emotion of the moment. Those situations call for a measured rather than decisive response.

At other times a decision has to be made quickly, usually to protect the safety of an individual in a community or the community as a whole. Later we can revisit the decision.

When a student was found in a pool of blood in her room, as a result of cutting her arm, the dorm parent called 911 and the ambulance was quickly there (the fire station is literally 150 yards from the dorm). The physical damage to the girl was not as serious as it first appeared, but clearly this was a situation that demanded some immediate response. Systemically, that decision was fairly easy, and it was a medical/psychological decision rather than a disciplinary one. Her parents had to come and take her home. They lived several states distant, but until they arrived the girl had to stay under the direct supervision of our medical staff. When or if she could return would necessitate a great deal of evaluation and consultation, and that would not be my decision. However, I would be part of the process and would have input.

The community is always distressed by such an action on the part of one of its members, and leadership requires taking that distress into account when the decision is made. We never seem to be able to escape that tension between the need to do what is best for the individual and what is best for the community; and we shouldn't.

Another similar situation, although involving alcohol, led me to a phone call to a parent as his son was preparing for the prom. The boy prepared by bringing a 30 pack of beer to his dorm room and sharing it with a couple of friends. He was caught because a dorm parent walking by heard a funny sound that he investigated. It turned out to be the sound of empty beer cans being crushed.

The parent was furious on the phone, first at another member of the administration who was carrying the walkie-talkie at the time, and then at me as the Dean. The outrage was palpable; the volume of the conversation on the walkie-talkie and phone hurt my ears. Not only could the boy not attend the prom, he would have to go home. How could I ruin a boy's career for drinking a beer? Didn't I ever do something like that? He had paid for the limo and prom tickets, etc. The fury reflected some other issue with that parent, but I managed to survive the episode. The parent came and picked up the boy and did not seek me out, rather unobtrusively taking the boy home.

Contrasted with that parent were the parents of another boy in the room who had been on Probation earlier in the year for drinking and knew that he would be dismissed if another similar situation arose. Those parents immediately came to the school, had a sad but frank conversation with me, held the boy accountable for his own behavior, and took him home, withdrawing him from school three weeks from graduation. I then had to work with the college which had accepted him and to which I had written a letter of recommendation to see how they would treat his matriculation even though he was not going to receive a diploma. He was fortunate; they decided they would allow him to come. And this was perceived to be a highly competitive, elite, small, liberal arts institution that highly valued character and community. Many at our school were surprised they allowed him to attend.

The buck stayed on my desk in those situations. The Dean of Discipline, Authority, Leadership and Stewardship.

WHAT IS IT WORTH?

I recently heard that former New York Mayor Rudolph Giuliani would get perhaps $100,000 per speech. Sometimes I think I could give as good a speech, and I would probably be happy with $50 and lunch. Some actors command $20 million to do a picture. I have been on stage plenty of times, but even with that background and at the age where I could probably only do character roles, I know I would not deserve even a small percentage of that rate. One percent of that would be only $200,000, but I doubt I could get that for even a good performance. I also don't belong to the union.

Although I only went to a small Division III college, I did play two varsity sports for four years each. Certainly I would not have gotten a second blink for anything beyond that, but I liked to dream about $100 million for a decade to play some entertaining game. My father was a legitimate baseball talent 70 years ago, but circumstances worked against him, and he did not get the break in the '30's that others would get now. What if . . . ? But then I wouldn't be who I am today.

At the end of the 1990's corporate executives were earning 419 times as much as industrial workers who were their employees (serfs?). $20,000 x 419 = . . . $8, 380,000. That is per year.

We all complain about how much the plumber or electrician makes when he or she comes to our house, especially on an emergency basis, but these are experts and we need them. We do not ordinarily complain about how much the pre-school, kindergarten or elementary school teacher makes. Having two of those-aged children at home, I know these teachers are not making enough! In 1999, the average annual salary for educators of early childhood or pre-school kids was $15, 430.

But what is the difference? We can put monetary value on the material things we need in our house, the advertising revenues and other revenues from a full arena or stadium, and the dividends from the stocks in our corporations. And Giuliani has been at the center of some crucial decisions that affected millions of people. He was "there," he has insight from his experience, but $100,000 for a speech? That's only the market value; somebody—and more than one—will pay it.

Are those teachers of the pre-teen and even pre-school children creating wealth? Certainly not in the short term, and as many have pointed out the United States has suffered grievously from the short-term view. The rebelliousness of the '60's was characterized by some very egocentric behavior as well as some vital social commitment to social justice for African-Americans, women, native-Americans and eventually gays. The '70's was dubbed the Me Generation. Generation X was succeeded by Generation Y, and booms and busts of the '80's and '90's had major critics of business practices and social and personal behavior. The critics cut across the entire political spectrum.

The products of those pre-teen years are my job as Dean, and while there is no guaranteed formula for creating that wonderful teenager who turns into a wonderful adult, there are some steps that will almost ensure that some of them will come through my door involuntarily. For students at risk in my school it is more often what parents do not do in the affective area rather than what they in fact do in the behavioral area. Parents of my charges have not beaten their children, financially or physically neglected them, or abandoned them. They more than likely would have substituted material goods for emotional connection, entitlement for earning, self-centered behavior for social commitment. The kids become alienated, disaffected, and lonely. Rather than to gang violence or other criminal behavior these kids turn to drugs, anti-social but not necessarily criminal behavior, the isolation of the computer world, or other high-risk activity. Then I might get to know them better.

While many people who know my job do not envy it, I

sometimes reflect on those who have similar jobs in schools or villages with teenagers who do not have the advantages that the teens in my school have. The teenagers I work with usually have a mother and father, not always together nor necessarily working in concert.

All families are dysfunctional, each in its own way. What is normal? No longer the nuclear group with mother, father, children. Fifty-percent of marriages in the 1990's were predicted to end in divorce. The diversity of ethnic background, color, religion, economic status, and sexual orientation is both exciting and educationally valuable. It does require, however, tolerance and understanding. The norm for schools, and the village of my own school, is not the norm of my bias or the successful alternative situations. We use the word dysfunctional to describe the more extreme problems that we face, but I paraphrase Tolstoy's comment about happy and unhappy families: every family is dysfunctional, each in its own way. We are all at risk when we make judgments; our personal biases are always present.

I do not often have to work with violence. For that I am extremely grateful. Fear can paralyze both individuals and institutions. I would love to see that fear and its causes diminish dramatically in American society. Those who work directly with those issues have a much more challenging job than I have. I would love to think we did not need so many of those people, knowing that we do not even have nearly enough. There is still plenty of room for more psychologists, social workers, and family therapists.

We do not choose our parents. Every child, every teenager, deserves a caring environment. The child did not choose to have wealthy parents, bright parents, loving parents. The child did not choose to have neglectful, impoverished, or uneducated parents. While success, however one wants to define it, will come less often to the second group, failure or difficulty can also fall upon the first group.

Could I transfer my success or self-satisfaction from my working with the first group to the second group? Probably not. Middle-class, liberal, white male guilt aside, I do not have the training or perhaps the personality to work with the kids with those issues. (I also do not have the skills or inclination to work all the time with the pre-teen group!) Nevertheless, from time to time I do see some students at our school who have had a difficult background. They have overcome some serious disadvantages to arrive here. Some then succeed here; some do not.

Yet I am sure that if we as a society put as much money, energy, and care into looking for the future of children as we do for the material and social gains for ourselves, we would have fewer social problems, both at the individual and community level. "Don't give me your Sixteen-year old and say: Fix it." The teenager was broken a long time ago, not usually last year as a fifteen-year old.

It is not the Dean's job to find out what scar lays unattended from an injury early in a child's life. The emotional hole that begs for fill does not reveal itself simply by observation or even behavior. That is for the counselor or psychologist.

I know that we do not have enough of those skilled people available, and I know that if we as a society did more in the earliest years of children's lives that we would not need as many of them. Good nutrition, attention to reading, attention to music and art, physical exercise, love: they should not be introduced to a teenager as a first time experience. They should be part of the fabric of that person's life. No high school, no Dean, no college, no surgeon is going to implant those needs into a teenager.

We should not be surprised that teenagers aspire to the fame and wealth of their favorite rock stars or athletes. I doubt that they would aspire to Giuliani's speaking fees because they do not see the glamour there. They would enjoy the money, but they have a sense that he had to be involved in decision-making and difficult situations. The teenagers do not see those difficulties in Halle Berry's career, or Madonna's, or Michael Jordan's. They think these stars simply have talent, but most importantly they have status. They have glitter and gold. They have fame, but even I could get at least Andy Warhol's celebrated fifteen minutes worth with the right break. So thinks the teenager.

That is not all bad. And certainly not all teenagers feel that way. But that is the image we are presented daily in the media, and what has value for us is often what we are taught. And what we are taught in those years long before teenage-hood and hormonally charged adolescence will be the foundation for future success.

The kindergarten teacher poster girl is a contradiction of value. Nevertheless, it is the kind of image we somehow need to celebrate and reward. We also need to give help, recognition, and support to adults in families. Parents have a tough job, and despite all the wonderful "how to" books that are out there, there is a tremendous amount of on-the-job learning.

Certainly the growth of contact between the Dean and his office mates with parents has increased steadily in the last decade. In addition to the benefit in communication, the opportunity to share our own village values with people who do not live here increases our commitment to shared values. Frankly, it also helps us prevent problems that are common with teenagers and it gives us opportunity and support for intervention. It also has helped us provide strength in numbers for what usually are shared values.

We have occasionally had discussion groups for parents so that we can talk as a community of adults about our common concerns. Parents are not only looking for information and advice, they are also looking for support from their peers. When peers gather to share information and stories they most likely will find that they are not alone with their concerns. Many parents are embarrassed or ashamed of what their children have done; many are worried about what their children might do; many are unaware of what their children are in fact doing. The first group is reluctant to share, the second group is anxious to the point of distraction, the third group is smug or naïve, politely willing to listen while thinking they have nothing to add.

At one meeting I blithely relayed the hypothetical situation where the parents went off to their house on Martha's Vinyard for the weekend, leaving their mature teenage child or children in charge of the house. When they returned they discovered that something approaching Animal House had occurred in their nice suburban home. After the meeting two parents approached me and asked if I was talking about them. I was not, but apparently I could have been. We had a nice discussion and they felt they had had a good learning experience. It turned out that they in fact had more to learn in the coming years, but then again so did I.

A year after another boy's graduation, I was finally told the story of how he had had such a party at his home when a sophomore or junior. In addition to well-appointed furniture and furnishings, the house also contained a valued and extensive wine cellar that was discovered by the partygoers. From a small gathering of perhaps ten friends, the group had quickly grown to perhaps 50 or a 100. I'm sure the number will grow as the lore gets passed through the ranks of storytellers. I was given the image of a teenager happily swilling from a $100 bottle of wine.

While I am sure the parents were more than a little unhappy about the damage done to their home—I think I remember $30,000 as a figure quoted to me, but that is probably hyperbole—I am not surprised they did not enlist the sympathy or support of the school. After all, it was on the weekend, the boy was a day student, and they probably did not know who was at the party. And it was no doubt none of my business.

Although I do not remember the context in which I was told the story, I do remember the particular student. He had been in my class as a senior. He was an average student (remembering that means he was college-bound and capable of solid academic achievement), but he did make one small impression on me. We have classes on Saturdays, about every other one, and half the classes would meet on each of those Saturdays. So I would see him once a month on a Saturday. I am also a teacher who gives frequent quizzes, usually based on the reading and designed to reward those who do the regular work. I give quizzes that can earn 120 points (grade inflation with a standard based on 100!), so that the student who misses a day of work, because there was a paper due or a big test in another class or an important NFL game the night before, can recoup the low grade by consistency the rest of the time. If there are fifteen quizzes in the semester it is not hard to have a good quiz average. Sometimes I have students angry because they only received 100 instead of 120, but that is a discussion of expectations that belongs later. Usually, however, the quiz average ends up being not too different from the test average or the overall average in the class. "A" students will usually do "A" work in all areas, "C" students "C" work in most areas, although they probably have more inconsistency than the best students. Certainly there are some whose grades will be lowered or raised by the quiz average, but I usually count it as 10-15% of a quarter's grade, hardly a GPA buster.

However, on that particular Saturday I gave a quiz. The young man told me it was Saturday and he didn't "do" quizzes on Saturday. I said, "fine" but that I did "do" quizzes, and he gave me the unanswered question back. He did not think the zero for the quiz was fair, which I agreed with on the basis that nothing in life is "fair," like my birth, my death, or his presence in my class, but the zero was simply the consequence for not taking the quiz. He then wanted a makeup quiz. All this discussion took place in the context of the class so the other sixteen or eighteen students had an opportunity to voice an opinion. Despite the fact that this was my elective course on Hitler and Nazi Germany, and that the authoritarian personality is part of our discussion as we look at the man and the era, the student found no allies in the class, and not because the students feared repercussions from the teacher. The student simply was arguing from a self-interested, self-centered position that made no rational sense to the rest of the class.

His parents were nice people, supportive of their children, interested in what was best for them, and respectful of teachers and what they were trying to do. But I suspect they would have benefited from more support from other parents and the school in the long-term growth of their children. The link between that incident and the party at his house is at best circumstantial, but it certainly is instructive in showing that multiple incidents of such nature should be cause for concern. However, that boy was already seventeen when he was in my class. Something did not quite register for him many years earlier.

He may turn out to be a fine adult. He will probably become a parent. What patterns will be repeated, which will be broken? I'm just curious.

Another example with another outcome occurred a year or so later. I was on duty for the weekend, and I was hearing rumors about a party, about kids being other than where they said they were supposed to be. So after dinner on a Saturday night I began calling parents. One lied to me at first about her son being home for the weekend. One would give me nothing but vague information that her daughter was not home where she said she would be but that she knew where she was, and a third thought that her daughter could not possibly be where she was rumored to be because the daughter had just called on the cell phone and said she was 20 miles in the opposite direction. The third parent decided to do some further checking; she was not naïve and wanted to be sure her daughter was safe.

The third parent discovered, by getting in her car and driving to a site, that her daughter was in fact hosting a party that had just begun. The party ended, she took charge of her daughter and the consequences. The first parent reluctantly came to the realization that we had responsibilities and commitments and that her child needed to be where he said he was going to be. If he went home, where he said he was going, and then went someplace else, that was the parent's responsibility and not ours. That student did not go home, and he did not want to tell the school where he was going—because he was going to the party. He eventually found another student's home to go to.

The second parent had no further interest in involving the school.

The disciplinary consequences for the students varied and were not what they might have been. Embarrassed as she might have been, the parent of the third student acted immediately and judiciously. She was able to see what the problem was, where responsibility lay, and what she had to do.

I certainly had plenty of work to do at the beginning of the next week, including listening to student assessment of the entire incident and hearing about comparisons to other incidents that had different resolutions. "It was all so unfair!" Indeed it was.

Nevertheless, the communication with parents, by parents, and among parents was an important part of the entire incident. Focusing more on that than the student activities gave us all the opportunity to learn what we need to do as parents and adults. And we still have to do it every year.

Placing a monetary value on parenting or educating hardly seems appropriate or even feasible, but we all place a value of some kind on those roles. Some things cannot be identified conveniently in dollar signs.

WORTH TOWARDS
SELF-WORTH

When we add an s to the word value we shift the discussion from economics to philosophy and ethics. Sometimes the shift seems like a leap. In our increasingly multicultural and diverse world, I find myself more conscious that I may have different assumptions about both behavior and belief than the parents or students I am talking with. And they certainly have differences within their own groups.

Good communication with and among parents also helps us prevent problems that are common with teenagers. That communication also gives us opportunity and support for intervention. Additionally, it has helped us provide strength in numbers for what usually, although not always, are shared values.

We do not always share the same commitment to the same values when they affect us personally. A good example is honesty. We iterate in our publications, our speeches, our classrooms that honesty with each other and with ourselves gives us integrity, that sense of wholeness that makes us who we are.

And yet each of us lies and deals with lying every day. We might lie to gain something. We might lie to avoid losing something. As much as it may sound like the bugaboo that people refer to as situational ethics, there are indeed some lies that are worse than others.

Several years ago our frustration both as individuals and as an institution representing us, led us to make lying a Major Rule violation, punishable at least by Probation. We had for years before then included the idea that lying in front of the Discipline Committee would be grounds for Dismissal, that is, a student would leave the school with no hope for return. That seemed logical; if a student was going before the Discipline Committee and had any hope of leniency then lying would indeed be foolish. And yet it occurred from time to time, usually because a student had the fear of Dismissal anyway and was willing to gamble individual integrity in hopes of an extraordinary piece of good luck. And I have no doubt that it has been, on occasion, successful.

I would venture that our student population is more aware now, in comparison with a decade ago, of the commitment the school is making to honesty in our academic and personal relationships. While I have been writing this book about our community, students in particular have been trying to find some reason how they can be in it. I guess it is part of the 15 minutes of fame phenomenon, but it has been interesting to gather more details of stories and even more stories themselves by encouraging current and former students to talk. Some think I am going to focus exclusively on the difficult issues, on the problems that kids had. Perhaps they want me to put a favorable spin on a story, perhaps they just want to know they have been included, even though I have said "no names."

In one casual conversation I had with a boy and his much younger girl friend, he wanted me to include an incident that I had forgotten about. It was a typically freshman/sophomore experience. One boy had borrowed, without permission, another boy's bike and had had an accident that damaged the bike. He then decided that he might as well deliberately destroy the bike further through more conscious abuse. By the time he and the bike were back at the dorm, the owner had recognized the futility of trying to restore the bike and decided to join in with the abuse. (I somehow missed the rationale of how he arrived at that point.) Four boys then decided that they would play a game of launching the bike from the second floor to the ground and repeating the process, presumably until it stopped being fun. However, a neighboring dorm parent emerged and it became immediately clear that the game would be over. The boy telling me the story said that he saw the dorm parent coming and left the first floor, his station in the game, to leave the scene. Alas, he was questioned and he decided to admit what he knew. Part of why he did that was because of recent Probations for lying, he said. No one had broken any rules, but they certainly realized that they were doing something that was going to get them unwanted attention from adults.

I asked him why he thought I should include that story in my book. Under what theme would it go? He was not sure but just thought it was a good example of silliness that went on but that he was glad that he had told the truth. In the grand scheme of things a minor anecdote. Not that he had been clear of other trouble along his way, but he was the only one of the four boys still in the school. I told him that fact might be worth a note. Was his basic good character an important factor in his ability to negotiate the difficult path of adolescent maleness? I decided to leave the conversation with that on his plate. His girl friend was confident he would graduate, and he knew he did not have much wiggle room if he encountered further trouble.

If honesty is a character trait we value highly, it is also one we are not easily going to install in an adolescent's personality machine. We may be able to reinforce it or enhance it, but if it is not there when the student arrives, the student has a high risk of not completing the educational opportunities at the school.

Most people, and undoubtedly teenagers at a higher rate, would be quick to tell a lie when first confronted about an issue; it seems almost automatic. ("What is that beer can doing under your bed?" says the adult. "What beer can?" says the student? Or, "I didn't know that beer can was there!") Now, any defense lawyer would probably claim this statement of a lie was inadmissible evidence, but we are not yet in court. I am also talking here about the issue of honesty not the specific case about the beer under the bed, but I thought I would use an image that many dorm parents, as well as real parents, would appreciate.

The reaction lie is different from the calculated lie. An example of the latter would be the student who went to Health Services to claim illness as an excuse to stay there rather than go to class, and when questioned as to whether or not there was a test in that class says "No" . . . when in fact there is a test. While we still have those incidents, we have honed our skills of asking the right questions. We still can hear a "I forgot we had a test" and that could conceivably be true, but the calculated lie seems to have diminished over the years.

While we all struggle with the complexities of life and often pine for the simplicity of the good old days—which of course never existed—the teenagers struggle more. They need to know more information and we need to be ready to help them get it. With the illness at Health Services, they need to know that if they are genuinely sick they can indeed be excused from the test until they are healthier. If they are just tired because they stayed up all night studying, then they are not ill. They should take the test and then go to Health Services—or back to bed and take the consequences of an absence.

Foresight is not a strength of the teenager, and that is connected to the physical development of the brain itself, incomplete even yet for the teenager.

Sometimes students simply need a little extra help, patience from an adult, to see that there are consequences to actions. The teenager may not like the answer he or she is forced to give to the questioner, but it is an important process. Teenagers accept responsibility; they are not amoral. They just sometimes need a little more help.

It is uncomfortably more frustrating when the parents conspire with the teenagers to help them avoid consequences. While boarding students have to negotiate through a professionally trained nurse to have their health status diagnosed, commuting students might only have to sway a sympathetic parent. We have students who have a higher rate of absentee excuses on days when there are tests and papers than on other days. Sometimes the parent calls are just pro forma: the student is ill and will not be in school today. Some struggle with their dilemma and choose to rationalize both for themselves and with the school. Is it in fact ok to miss morning classes, one of which includes a test or a quiz, because the student did not get to bed until late because he attended a pro football Monday night game? Is it fair to that student to be at a disadvantage for the test because he was tired? Is it fair to others who did not go to the game and who therefore might get a comparatively higher grade? This might be the one factor that prevents the student from making the Honors or Cum Laude list or the final cut to the college of his choice. And how often might the opportunity for this game, or the Super Bowl or the Final Four or the Frozen Four, all of which have happened for us at school, come along? These are tough choices sometimes, and who is going to determine what the consequences should be? Values and authority cohabit the shadowy world of our ethical behavior.

Lower on the order of miscues are latenesses, and sometimes the stories here are cuter. We were late to school because my son had to finish his college essay after breakfast. My daughter was late because she was tired. My son was late to first period because he had to take the trash out to the end of the driveway, which is quite a distance from the house. All actually are true incidents.

And indeed kids are different from each other. So are parents. One parent called me in exasperation because she could not get her son out of bed and she herself had to go to work. She was tired of being late and was looking for advice. I suggested she leave him, making sure that he knew she would not give him an excuse and that he could suffer the consequences. She seemed comfortable with that plan, and sure enough a couple of days later she called me from work to say that she had left him and that he would not be in. I told her I would call him.

A bit later I called him—about ten—and woke him up. He was chagrined but understood. I offered to pick him up (he lived about ten minutes away), so that at least he would not miss his last two classes and the JV soccer game in the afternoon. He said ok, and I drove out to get him. We had a nice conversation on the way back, he was grateful, and I don't think he missed another day for quite some time.

Now this scenario could not always take place. I do not simply sit at my desk and wait for such moments to occur, but the timing was serendipitous and I no doubt won future points with both student and parents—and others that they would talk with. Perhaps someone will argue that I am enabling this student. However, teenagers need this extra effort from not only their overstressed parents but from others in the community. The good village works this way.

There has been a revival of talk about character education and the development of character the last several years. For a while the idea reigned that that character development belonged in the home or the church but not in schools, and anyone suggesting that we talk about character would open the Pandora's box of values. With cultural diversity and emphasis on sensitivity towards difference, schools were reluctant to take a firm position. Gradually, schools began to focus more on individual behavior, demanding that students and adults be held accountable for their behaviors. Past history, personal and social circumstances, or a medical condition like A.D.H.D. were no longer going to be used as excuses for behavior that went against school rules.

These changes in emphasis did not require a dramatic difference in tone, not a crusade against a declining civilization, organizations like the Moral Majority notwithstanding. The pendulum swung more towards an individualism that included people being responsible for their own actions while at the same time lauding them for reaching their own potentials. But if we could take credit for successes, then we also had to take responsibility for our failures. By 2002 the effort to place blame on someone or something for failure was receiving little tolerance.

As we have moved both as a school and as a society towards more commitment to community and less towards the elevation of the individual, we have affirmed our ideal that the two reinforce each other. The European tax structure has a more explicit "value added" tax, a tax that goes on to every product as the product moves from inception to final use. If the value increases by some process there is a tax on that process. Similarly, when the individual improves and grows then the value of the entire community benefits, a value add-on rather than a tax.

If the community grows and improves, the ideal would be that everyone in that community would grow, but that has not been the case on the national level in the United States. There are a great many people who have not benefited by American economic growth, personally as well as financially. On the village level, on the level of the school as a community, growth benefits are more easily shared. But teaching character on the more impersonal national level cannot compare with teaching character on the village and family level.

Civic virtue is an old concept, talked about by Socrates and even earlier Greek philosophers, talked about by the early leaders of the young United States. Civic virtue was a fundamental component of educational efforts in the first decades of the new republic. Writers even made it a focus of their works. In my US History classes I always enjoyed talking about Mason (popularly known as Parson) Weems' biography of George Washington where he introduced us to the chopping-down-the-cherry tree story. The specific purpose for the story was to establish character in the nation's first President. Truth was not as important as character for the good of the nation, and generations of youth grew up with that myth. I am beginning to lose my surprise now when I hear that American teenagers have not heard that story of the cherry tree. I guess because it was not true it is no longer taught. Yet I think the value espoused is worth keeping the tale alive, not as truth but as a commitment to a value that Americans still believe in: honesty. With teenagers, telling them the story still has merit if their ability to distinguish between myth and reality is developed. However, if their character has not already been developed, trying to implant a sense of honesty as a cherished value will not likely take root in the high school years.

The older students, and perhaps even the younger ones, might point out that lying was ok in the context of the cherry tree story. The absolutists would have difficulty justifying it because it indeed was lying; and lying is wrong.

I prefer history classes to ethics classes to discuss ethical problems. My bias is with an academic discipline that focuses on real events in difficult situations. Not that ethics classes do not do that; I just prefer coming at it from a different direction. The danger is that we justify illegal and immoral acts by the outcome produced.

We will also as adults be smattered with the hypocrite label. It's ok, students say with a scornful sneer, for the adults to lie but not the students. Sometimes we adults simply have to lie to protect some other more important truth. That is also true for students.

A senior girl had been sexually assaulted several days earlier, and for several days she struggled with what to do. When she finally confided to someone who then involved an adult, she made it clear that she was willing to talk with Health Services personnel and me, but that we were not to inform her dorm parent. She had to lie to him to protect what she felt would be confidentiality issues. In the grand scheme of things, this lie was not particularly crucial because she did tell people who *should* know. Her issue of truthfulness revolved more around a personality conflict, and she simply wanted to keep distance between herself and the dorm parent. I am not sure anyone would put that in the category of lying in an immoral sense.

Students have pleaded with me not to tell their parents about some issue, but I tell them that if it is a formal disciplinary issue I must inform the parents. This brings up the can't/won't distinction. "You can't tell my parents." "I can't tell my parents; they'll kick me out of the house (or worse)." "I can't tell you . . ." These statements all incorrectly use can't when they mean won't. I can't dunk a basketball on a normal basketball court. There is a reality there that is not going to happen. "Can't" in the above situations is used to avoid making the hard choice, dealing with the difficult consequence.

History provides us with enough examples of breaking the law and lying to keep the ethicists at work. The examples that I have used in my classes—the development of the United States Constitution, Lincoln's leadership in the Civil War, and Germany's bombing raid on the city of Coventry in 1940—give me good discussion material. However, I think students need to know facts about the incidents, the contexts of the events, and the reasoning behind the decisions made. Then we can get to the ethical dilemmas.

Hopefully briefly, because this is about me as Dean dealing with values and not me as history teacher, I argue that the Constitution would not have been possible had their not been secrecy and confidentiality in the negotiations to bring forth a new document to replace the constitution the country had had for six years, known as the Articles of Confederation. The 55 delegates to the Constitutional Convention in Philadelphia used a device called the Committee of the Whole to exclude non-members of the Congress, meaning specifically the press. Then they could get to the necessary compromises to bring the thirteen squabbling states, two major regions—North and South—and competing egos to come to an agreement that would benefit the whole even if some of the parts had to sacrifice.

Although there were a number of compromises, I will use one for the discussion of ethics. How could intelligent, articulate, well-read leaders agree that a group of people could be counted as three fifths of a person? Should a slave be viewed as a human being with rights and privileges, "all men are created equal," or simply a piece of property? They haggled until they developed the three fifths Compromise: slaves were counted as three fifths of a man but could not vote and certainly had no means of paying what citizens called taxes. There were few abolitionists in 1787, but should they have held fast to no compromise and possibly sacrifice the hope of a stronger union of the states? In the context of 1787, this was not going to happen, but in the 21st century it is certainly easier pass judgment on the moral question. In the 22nd century will people be passing similar judgment on the United States' response to 9/11?

Seventy-five years after the adoption of the Constitution the country was at war with itself, with the immediate cause the right of states to secede from the Union, and the pervading problem of slavery underlying all issues at stake. Abraham Lincoln, elected with a majority of electoral votes but a plurality of the popular votes (his opponents together had more popular votes than he did), faced many choices whenever he had to make a decision. He exercised more power than he was constitutionally allowed, but that seems to be less important to us 150 years later than the fact that he guided the country through the four years of turmoil and set it on the path to reconciliation. His exercise of power is judged by the outcome. He bent the Constitution so that it would not break.

In my Hitler and Nazi Germany class I have sometimes told the story and sometimes had the class play roles to come to a conclusion on the problem of the German bombing of Coventry in November of 1940. The problem was that Winston Churchill knew that the bombing raid was going to happen because his code breakers had translated German communications. If he had warned the people of Coventry and had alerted the military to take more direct action more people in Coventry would have survived the bombing, but the Germans probably would have realized their code had been broken. Should Churchill have saved some in 1940 at the risk of sacrificing many more later on or even losing the war altogether?

Most students do not like the position Churchill took. Sitting in the secure classroom 60 years later, with the Nazis defeated and the United States and its allies and values triumphant, shouldn't there have been some way both to save the people of Coventry and protect the secret of the discovery?

Philosophers have struggled with these issues as well, trying to come up with a system or a universal law. Sometimes, as I learned when I took on the History of Western Philosophy course, we follow Kierkegaard's idea that we simply have to take "a leap of faith." We cannot prove God's existence, at least not with the certainty that medieval philosophers did, in the face of scientific achievements over the last centuries. At some point believers must rely on faith.

We struggle through Kant and his contributions to modern moral philosophy. Even though we have appetites and fears (some irrational or even evil), should there not be a universal law as to how we should act?

"Kant says that when we act in a way that we would want without contradiction everyone else to act, then it is a '*universal law*,' which no government has the right to deny. To pin down what he means, he describes behavior that while defensible, could not be made universal without grave contradictions: "Consider a man whose life is full of troubles that lead him to despair. Knowing, therefore, that in all probability the future holds more unhappiness than happiness, he decides out of self-love to kill himself. While justifying such an action, Kant notes that suicide could not be a universal law because the general purpose of life cannot be to destroy itself.

Consider another man who needs to borrow money in order to survive, but knows that he can never repay it. Out of desperation, he borrows the money anyway. But if everyone were to do that, Kant says, then no one would lend money anymore. So it could not be a universal law.

Finally, consider a man in fortunate circumstances who just wants to be left alone, and so does not help or harm those in dire need. But even he, Kant explains, cannot wish, without contradiction, for everyone always to act thus, since there would be moments in life when he would require the goodwill of others." (Kaplan 111,112)

I will return to the above quote and its setting in the section on Politics, yet how many eighteen-year olds are familiar with these struggles? How many adults are? For the teenagers, the importance of here and now reigns supreme, even if they are vaguely planning for an event next Saturday night. As I struggled through my toddlers' years I learned more fully about the concept of time. It's really quite easy. There is Now and Not Now. Teenagers are able to expand considerably on that. They do understand Then and Later, but understanding does not mean these two concepts are the governing forces in decision-making.

Related are the Concrete and the Abstract. The classroom activity, the dorm meeting, the proctor meeting—they all provide good training for the mind. Applying that abstraction of discussion and debate to the concrete world takes both training and time.

How do students know the teachers are telling the truth? How does a student know that he can trust me? Those are abstractions made concrete by experience. How many of us have been victimized by the fast-talker, the smooth operator? Hopefully we learn through experience.

My success as Dean must rely on faith from those I work with. I do not expect unquestioned faith, but I must have far more of it than its opposite. Nevertheless, I have some battle scars. The following was in response to an incident that involved alcohol and several students.

In your letter to the [the parents], you state: "The community will have members who feel justice was not served and that integrity was not upheld. However, I believe that is how it will have to be. Individuals move on, both physically and emotionally, and the institution remains." I am responding as a member of the community who believes that your decision to not pursue this case is educationally unsound. While the students will move on and the institution will remain, I believe that the students have not learned that integrity and honesty are important moral and educational concepts, and the remaining institution has been weakened because of it.

The reasons you give for not requiring [the student] to appear in front of the Discipline Committee are vague and confusing. You state that his appearance would "add more negative energy to an already painful situation." It seems to me that while this might be the case, an important lesson could be learned through this negativity and pain. The negativity of the situation is rooted in [the two boys'] inability to tell the full truth. You state that "the full truth is not apparent, and at least one, if not more, of the boys must be lying." What lesson do [they] learn when we decide to ignore this "impasse"? Is it educationally sound to avoid situations that are negative and painful? It seems to me that by not having [the boy] appear before the Discipline Committee (like {the other one}did), we are sending, a message to the boys and the community that we are only willing to pursue discipline cases that are easy to understand and enforce. I am aware of the complexities of the case: they are seniors; [one] seems unstable and may explode if he is pushed (like he did in your office); we are busy with the various end-of-the-year commitments we all have. Yet, by not pursuing the truth and justice in this case, aren't we implicitly condoning [his] violent outburst? His vehement denial "worked"; he does not have to confront himself and the community with this issue anymore. Is this the lesson we want [him] to learn?

*Moreover, in [the other boy's] Discipline Committee meeting, we stated clearly that if he were found to be lying, his "discipline" would change from a suspension to a dismissal; now you admit that he may be lying but refuse to pursue the truth. What message does that send to [him]l? We tell him during the meeting that it is imperative that he tell the truth, but now we are showing him that it was just an empty threat. We are telling him and the community that the truth is only important to pursue when it is convenient and easy. Finally, it doesn't make sense for you to state that the students are probably lying, and then conclude that the students' consciences will "do [their] proper work." By dropping this issue now, we are modeling for the students that it is better to avoid hard questions if they are not neat and clean, yet we are confident that the students will themselves struggle with **these hard questions** on their own? That seems very unrealistic.*

*This incident is another example of [the school] taking a soft stand on integrity and honesty. Two years ago, we voted to make lying, a major school rule violation; however, we have condoned lying in Discipline Committee meetings twice this quarter. I remember reading in the **write-up of the . . . meeting** [with three other students] that the **Committee felt that they***

were all lying, but they were not punished for their violations.
This incident is similar. While we may be enabling a few seniors
to graduate . . . , we are sending a terrible message to both them
and the community. We are teaching the seniors that lying helps
them avoid responsibility for their actions and the subsequent
punishment, and we are teaching the community that our beliefs
and rules are dubious and hypocritical.

As [a] dorm head . . . next year, I am planning to emphasize
honesty, integrity, and communication. [the school]'s pattern of
avoiding conflict and condoning, lying worries me, greatly. If
the Dean of Students doesn't uphold the school rules and
emphasize the importance of integrity, the rest of us who do are
undermined.

cc:[Discipline Committee Chair, Head, Assistant Head,
Assistant Dean, another faculty member on the Committee]

These are the kinds of situations and follow-ups that drive deans to other jobs.

Nevertheless, that faculty members exercise such energy over issues like this, which are not every day occurrences, is healthy rather than unhealthy. It is good to have faculty members who value integrity. I'll lose my job if my boss feels I lack the integrity he wants in his Dean, but he and I and others know I will continue to make errors in judgment. While I cannot make too many, it is inevitable I will make a few.

The student in question failed out of college after his first semester. We had some success with him for three years. Something went wrong somewhere, and while I developed some pretty good guesses late that spring maybe I did take the easy way out; maybe I took the wise way out. Baseball is such a good microcosm of American values. If a hitter consistently bats .350 he has a good chance of getting into the Hall of Fame. A fielder must be closer to .990 to win plaudits. I wonder what a good Dean's percentage should be out of every 1000 students?

I really do not have many letters that I have kept that I can cite as evidence for various issues, but I do have a couple of student ones that help balance the critical ones I have received from parents and faculty members. Although I should have edited the following brief email to make it look better to the critics, I will just include it as I received it.

> *My visit last weekend was short. I never got to ask you how your son was doing, and how your late nights were treating you. My late nights treat me pretty good, although they are not spent enjoying what many call "The college Experience" they are filled with the likes of Langston Huges, line memorizing and countless cups of JAVA. I have nothing to gain, material wise, now that I am an alumni not a student, by saying this, but you certainly made an impact upon me during my two year career at [school]. I thought that it was proper for me to give you thanks and praise for that. I am not sure what is was. Maybe because you insist on knowing each student by name, or that you understand that each problem has a oulution that can be talked through. Keep it up. By God don't retire soon, what ever wing nut they get to headmaster next will need you to keep students in line. I am afraid that [college] is not the place I envisioned it to be. Maybe because downtown is filled with 56 bars, and everyones main objective is to see if they can cram all of them in, within their freshman year. Rather than craming for tests. I prefer the cheap beer. A little alumni humor. But in all seriousnees, I am glad that I had the . . . experience, but also regret it a little as well. If I was niave as some of these new students, it would be easy for me to float by and colect even more fat above my waits line. I guess there is responsibilty that comes along with new knowledge. Anywho, thank you so much and keep intouch.*

Several points in this letter are worthy of further discussion, as in, for example, the chapter on alcohol. But I survive as Dean because I view the job as process rather than end. There is responsibility that comes with new knowledge, and there will always be new knowledge. Both the teacher and the student quoted above believe in character; so too does the school.

Another theory for the existence of good character is that everyone is born with it, but some have lost it during their early years as a result of neglect and a lack of practice and re-enforcement. Perhaps a good village, new to the young person attending a new school, can reawaken that sleeping good character. Perhaps if the peer group is committed enough to what it thinks is good character then the dormant goodness in the person of weak or bad character will emerge.

It has been an interesting dilemma for parents as well as students to have to face the reality of an incident that involves character. One chooses whether to be honorable or dishonorable. The honorable act would be to acknowledge the deed and withdraw from the school if it were a dismissible offense. With the provisions we have for people to make mistakes and grow from them, having a second chance and perhaps given certain circumstances even additional opportunities, the choice to be dishonest is indeed that—a choice.

Having been at that table with the Head, Assistant Head, parents and student and seen the rationalization—if not outright prevarication—from students and parents in an effort to remain at the school, I appreciate the honesty and respect that goes with people of good character. I also believe people who do not have good character will eventually have to come to grips with that lack, even if they manage to remain at the school as a result of lying.

Theft and lying go hand in hand, both examples of character that communities do not like in their presence. When we had a case of theft from book bags, sadly a behavior that is more common than we would like at my school and I suspect at most others, we were able in this particular case to find other students who led us, a bit circuitously, to the thief. He, of course, denied it, both directly and in front of the Discipline Committee who did not for a moment accept his explanations. Nevertheless, the boy's parents did. Much to the dismay, frustration, and anger of most members of the community, the boy was given one more chance. I am not sure whether the boy's parents really believed him or simply wanted desperately to keep him at school and not have to bear the shame of his dismissal. They could not take the step to withdraw him. We did not pull the trigger and dismiss him. Weakness? Perhaps. Within a month he had broken another school rule, one with no opportunity for wiggle room—in this case smoking in a dormitory—and he was dismissed.

His character—or perhaps the lack of it—did him in. "I told you so; we would have been better off dismissing him when we had the chance and spared ourselves more frustration and anger at the leadership of the school if we had acted earlier." A common reaction voiced by many at the time, understandable and justifiable. It is now ancient history (perhaps three years old?), and we have had plenty of other woes since then to keep us working. I suspect this particular case will not register in the historical record of the school as a major blunder, perhaps not even part of student or faculty lore that will be recognized in some class's 25th reunion. And while faculty and some student anger was real and perhaps produced some self-examination on the part of school administrators, decisions were made by human beings and not by institutional formula. If it was a mistake to let this boy remain, which it probably was, it was based on hope for a character change, which would have led to behavioral change. For him such change did not happen, and the result was predictable and a relief, both for those who were certain he should have been dismissed earlier and for those of us where were hesitant and opted for "another chance." We were rid of someone who was a decidedly negative force in the school. In some ways, we gambled that he would fail again, which he did. His parents finally had to accept that he could not be at the school. It would have been worse had he not failed again and at the same time did not change his behaviors based on his character. Even then, had he smirked as he received a diploma, he would eventually fail in some other arena. The loss ultimately was his anyway.

I found it telling that the next summer he was working as a telemarketer.

Another incident that frustrated me, but which did not get to the Discipline Committee, was a question of two girls contesting that the other one was responsible for bringing alcohol into the dorm. Perhaps it did not get to the Discipline Committee because one girl was a former student, and thus perhaps a convenient scapegoat to provide cover for the current student. I could not compel the former student to testify and thought this was a personal issue that could be resolved by a meeting with the girls and their parents.

Because I was in contact with both students and their mothers, the former student was willing to come in and try to help resolve the issue. That could be a good sign of her innocence, but when we met with both girls and their mothers neither side budged about what was the truth. Since I had no official responsibility over the former student, and since the current student was already going to be convicted of possession of alcohol and there was some consequence to be applied, I decided not to pursue the issue further. Nevertheless, the sight of two students, backed by their respective mothers, saying the other was one was lying, was both uncomfortable and frustrating. Each had something to protect and I guess at least one was willing to bald-face lie about it; and for that matter, it is conceivable that both lied. All I know is that both could not be telling the truth.

And what role did each mother play in this? Did one counsel her daughter to lie? I have enough experience with parental collusion to know that lying (at least up to a point?), happens among the parents, and that our children learn a great deal from their parents.

I wonder if some day I will learn what in fact happened. As the song says: the truth will set you free; so if I ask or if individuals feel they want to clear their consciences then they will tell me. It is not so important to me, but it should be to them. I suspect that most people have confessed it somewhere. The practice of confession in the Catholic Church helps with forgiveness, and I use the source of the word scapegoat in my Hitler course to explain how originally that term was used for the village to start the new year with a clean conscience. The members of the community would gather around a goat selected from the herd, lay hands upon it, and let their individual sins from the past year flow into the goat. Then they let the goat leave the herd, escape, carrying the sins of the community with it: the escaped goat. The idea has clearly been perverted to laying blame on someone else, usually a group as we have come to know the term from the 20th century. The scapegoat has come to mean passing on the sins without the concomitant necessity of forgiveness and responsibility.

The examples of truthfulness in my school as village are rife as well. They are not as dramatic because they tend to involve confession to an individual rather than to a larger group. Telling the truth in a difficult situation is a personal challenge and is more easily, and I feel, more appropriately done to other individuals rather than to a group. I think forgiveness is a personal response and not an institutional response. People do not lie to institutions; they lie to individuals. Cheating on tax returns by lying is not the sin of lying; it is the crime of fraud. Deviance, deception, misrepresentation, cheating—these all can be done to an institution. I prefer to consider the lie personal.

One evening a group of students went to the neighboring city for an evening out. An opportunity to buy alcohol presented itself, and two members of the group of five purchased a bottle of vodka. They then encouraged the rest of the group to go for a walk, during which they produced the alcohol. One of the group chose not to drink, but she also felt she could not leave the group, both for her own protection as well as for theirs They were also responsible for her ride home. When they finally were able to secure a ride back to school—picked up by a day student in her car passing by while they were waiting for a cab—at least two of the group were quite drunk. They had to stop the car, and while that was happening a local police car came by and the officer decided to check on the situation. A chunk of this story belongs in another chapter, but the girl who had not been drinking was caught up in the net.

When I talked with her she was forthright about what had happened; she indeed was in the presence of alcohol, a Major Rule violation. I encouraged her to go to the Discipline Committee rather than sign a waiver accepting responsibility and the consequences because I felt there was room for a different response. She accepted that opportunity.

In the Committee hearing she repeated her story. She answered all the questions in such a way that the Committee did not doubt her truthfulness, and she had the support of her faculty adviser. The Committee agreed that she was technically guilty but the spirit of her actions—staying with her friends to make sure they were ok and being dependent on them at the same time—deserved a more measured response. They recommended that she not be punished for the rule violation, making clear to her that she did not want to be in that situation again. They agreed that she had no knowledge of the purchase of the alcohol, did not drink, and did not try to lie her way out of trouble.

Because she had absolutely nothing to gain by lying perhaps this is not the best example of the value of telling the truth, but everyone felt good about the situation, including those who were appropriately penalized for their own transgressions. The consensus was that justice rather than the law had been served.

I have had students face me in a situation involving an opportunity to lie and then tell me they did not want to lie to me. Perhaps this was a self-serving statement on their part, a valiant attempt to win sympathy from the Dean, but I truly believe that at least some of those confessions have been genuine. I believe there have been such genuine confessions to other adults in the community as well. On the other hand, I have known instances where a student will not tell the truth to a particular adult as a last gasp of defiance, as an opportunity to preserve what they feel is some dignity in the face of what they perceive as a blatant power play. Then they go and confess to someone else. I worry most about people who will look me straight in the eye and deliberately tell me a falsehood; they have something in their pathology that will follow them for a long time.

Most people will lie if they think they can get away with it or if they are simply reacting in a protective mode; I understand and accept the latter, at least until the individuals have been given the opportunity to reflect. Then they put themselves in real jeopardy. I have also found it much better to confront students when they are under the influence of some illicit substance and then again after they have regained their full faculties. The written statements obtained during the former investigation are good evidence to present at the latter; it is helpful for the students to see the difference. I do firmly believe that a good personal relationship with someone will have a positive impact on any statement, especially if it is done where there will not also be additional public humiliation. To me, that is double jeopardy, although I know there is sentiment for public displays of the guilty.

If teenagers can move towards a genuine sense of their own self-worth, then they will be much better prepared to enter the adult world with skills and self-confidence.

TELEVISION V. PHILOSOPHY?

Although the Internet by the 21st century has threatened to displace television as our number one concern for educators, the older medium still has its hold on both students and adults.

At our school we do not allow the television on in the common rooms in the dorms or in the Student Center until 5:30 in the afternoon during the week. Students are not allowed televisions in their own rooms, but with the personal computer accessible to almost everyone there is more than enough opportunity to escape reality and perhaps even relax.

We often decry the mindless nature of television, with people watching the box and utilizing little emotion or imagination. In a residential community watching television takes on a bit more of a social activity; students do not often watch television alone, certainly not as much as they might if they were in their own homes. There is also the necessity of some kind of social decision-making that must go on: what channel are we going to watch? That decision may cause some students to leave, leaving a homogeneous group to watch a particular show. The time restrictions have eliminated the daytime soap operas and even the shock shows that proliferated during the '90's, Jerry Springer perhaps being the most noteworthy. Evenings and weekends may have particular television sets turned to sports or MTV and kids can migrate around to where they may find their tastes accommodated.

More often, though, the televisions are the vehicles for the constant stream of videos that can entertain for hours on end. In the 21st century they are already being challenged by the new technology of DVD's, but in either case the proximity of a large video store—100 feet from my office—can satisfy the demands of our population. The store's business must drop significantly when we are not in session, even though they require a $20 deposit by students to get a video card. Students are not happy with that restriction; not all of them are blessed with huge amounts of available cash.

Personally, I spend a good deal of time, this year in particular, watching television in the evenings. My first year as Dean was the introduction of *NYPD Blue*, but I did not realize until later that *Law and Order* had been on since 1990, and that and its spin-offs are now favorite shows. I also like *Boston Public, West Wing, CSI, The Agency* and *The Practice*. Not only do I find them entertaining, I find many dilemmas presented that have relevance to my job. The ethical dilemmas that the shows struggle with sometimes have direct relevance, and I can empathize with both the problems and the potential solutions.

Of course, I am fond of telling students and colleagues that I watch some of these crime shows to hone my investigative skills so that I can better manage my village and be a better Dean. There is some truth to that statement. I also know that next year when I am not on a sabbatical, I will have more school-related work and that the TV shows will be a luxury rather than a routine. So I am trying to learn as much as I can now. Someone is no doubt saying: Get a Life! I, however, am *choosing*, not passively watching.

When *Boston Public* first came on I did not like it, thinking it was a great advertisement for the independent schools and highlighted the fears that the public had about our public educational system and some of the kids (and adults), that were in it. That was disturbing because I thought it focused on the failings in our society. If the public education system fails then the country fails. It seemed too easy to assault public education.

However, I stuck with it and found plenty of situations that I could empathize with and relate to. And there were plenty of positive statements about the dedication and commitment of some of the very best teachers to help teenagers. The other issues besides US History, or English, or math occupied a lot of the time and energy of teachers and administrators. Some people fell by the wayside, but new teachers stepped in. The human-ness of the school crept into focus from time to time.

We don't have a "dungeon" class at my school, the last stop for many students who have no interest in being in school. We do not have teachers assigned to the bottom ten percent of the student body that no one wants to deal with. But the bottom ten percent at my school is also in the top half of the *Boston Public* school. That is part of what may be perceived as the privilege of my school. Seeing some scenes and stories in that series keeps my own work in a perspective.

Week after week must be challenging to keep an audience both entertained and intellectually stimulated, and sometimes some of the vignettes or stories do not ring true or realistic to me. But then again, my job and daily work have the same sense of peaks and valleys, of positive efforts and foolishness, of excitement and routine. We struggle to keep students interested and involved in classes, their short attention spans increasingly mirrored in adult short attention spans as well (i.e., last decade's teenagers are this decade's new adults). So it is no surprise that every week's episode is not as good as I hope.

One particular episode I felt critical about was when the Principal's daughter reappeared on the scene, having left a prestigious independent boarding school. He had no idea of the reasons behind her expulsion. Unless one parent has legally prevented the other parent from receiving information about a student's performance at a private school, both parents receive copies of letters. And every school in this litigious age is going to be documenting actions taken against a student and sending copies to all parties.

While I know that parents sometimes are not in close contact with their children, not to know that your daughter had been in trouble on numerous occasions at a prestigious prep school struck me as unrealistic. Then followed a reconciliation that was sweet but not credible.

The shows that have featured the law have proliferated in the '90's, and while I have certainly not seen all of them, I am impressed with a movement towards the recognition of the complexity of life. Good versus evil, right versus wrong are constantly challenged by the complexities of cases. That, too, must be confusing for the younger elements in the audience. Teenagers in particular—though these shows are not aimed at them—are caught in the desire to have simple solutions to complex problems and frustrated by the absence of such solutions most of the time. On one hand, this desire/frustration experience contributes to the sliding scale of "truth" and the tendency to make relativity of values dominant over a clear delineation of right from wrong. On the other, it often demonstrates that what we see is not always what is true. The use of DNA testing in criminal cases has made its way to the crime shows, and now stories highlighting victims of misguided conviction are appearing. Sometimes, as well, the bad guys get through the system.

Fortunately, historians and history teachers can get through the rose-tinted glasses from time to time. Who did shoot Liberty Valence? *The Man Who Shot Liberty Valence* was a John Ford epic starring John Wayne and Jimmy Stewart. It includes the memorable line: When the legend becomes fact, print the legend.

One evening I received a call that some boys were late returning to study hall; I had no further information so I told the dorm parent we should wait a bit. They returned soon after, and one of them was bruised so the dorm parent suggested I come over. After I arrived, we decided we had better go to the Health Services where the nurse ministered to his bruises.

First I heard the story that the boys had been accosted in the neighboring town and that one of them had been sucker-punched for no apparent reason. Then there may have been some attempt to buy marijuana; and then there was a story that they had not called to say they were late because they thought they might get in trouble. Finally, they said a cab was late arriving to take them back. I said we should notify the police department there. The police said I should bring the three boys over for an interview.

I took out a school van and the four of us proceeded to the police station five miles away at nine PM in the middle of the week. We had a pleasant chat on the way and I expressed my concern for them as well as my interest in their tale. What was our nice little neighboring city coming to! Of course I knew that there were drugs available, that some sections of the town had congregations of alienated youth, and that college kids abounded because of several local colleges in the area. Not really much different, except perhaps for the number of college stunts, than most towns and cities in the United States.

My future career as an interrogator dimmed after our meeting at the police station. The boys were interviewed separately, and I continued to chat amiably with the other two as each took his turn. Finally it was my turn, and the detective said that nothing added up and that the kids were lying. We agreed on which of the three would be the easiest to break, and indeed he quickly recanted. The potential criminal charges by the police were not going to be worth the risk for the students or worth the time and bureaucracy for the police. The detective and I agreed that school punishment would be fine, compounded with other school penalties already imposed.

The boy who confessed first was on Probation at school. He had been cited recently for the "projectile" rule. He had thrown a snowball at a passing car. The car was driven by a police officer. This was not his winter! Throwing things at buildings or people, perhaps lacrosse balls or snowballs, is an endangerment to property and person, and we instituted the rule a few years before. It grew out of snowballs in the winter, and while willing participants in a snowball fight are ok, unwilling participants are seen as victims of a school-defined offense. It is not yet clear to me what happens when a willing participant gets injured, where responsibility will lie, how the injured party may sue the school for negligence, etc. That is part of the debate of law versus justice—the TV shows have managed to highlight that distinction as well—and part of me says we will just have to wait for the case. As hard as we try to prevent human foolishness, we never will be totally successful.

The story finally emerged as the other two students also decided truth was better than the lie. Their recent experience was pretty hard evidence that telling the truth and taking the consequences was not only more honorable but also legally preferable to the alternative—if, of course, you got caught. Places like Las Vegas thrive on that risk-taking behavior, but we like to think we can engrain some integrity in our youth, and that integrity will serve them well when they encounter all forms of risk-taking behavior, both the risks for gain as well as the risks for loss.

The three boys had gone to another school—nearly two hours by car—for the afternoon so that one of them could see his girl friend. The other two went for the ride. They had persuaded a fourth student, a day student who had a car, to drive them there. She did that, returned to visit her boy friend for a while, miscalculated the time crunch, and finally returned to pick them up to take them back to school. Her time on the road must have been seven hours.

On the way back they knew they were going to be late so they concocted a plan to explain their lateness. One boy told a second one to punch him in the face in the back seat of the car and they would use that as evidence for the story about being sucker punched in town.

They were perhaps a half hour late for evening study hall, not the most egregious offense in the books. They had not signed out properly as to where they would be that afternoon; if they were going to be out of town they needed to sign out in the dorm. Again, this was an offense worthy of penalty but not the threat of Dismissal. Yet they had enough accumulated minor offenses that they feared more serious punishment. So they risked fiction worthy of a TV show.

One of the boys went home on a medical leave; he was having personal difficulties in several areas, and this incident pushed him over the edge. Volunteering to get punched in the face would be good evidence of that. One withdrew from school, his parents exasperated at his persistent poor decision-making. He had been the one to first reveal the lie of the story. The parents were grateful for our efforts, and they knew that the responsibility for his behavior was on his shoulders. The third also withdrew, having been on Probation for possession and use of marijuana.

The driver of the car had done nothing illegal, but I did have a good conversation with her parents as well. Clearly her choice of using her unstructured time was not what her parents thought wise, and they took steps at home to address the issue that was indeed theirs and not the school's.

There are more chapters to this story, and no doubt more to come as the consequences continue to unfold. The boy who went on medical leave returned, had a successful senior year, and graduated in good standing with no further problems. He and his parents addressed the issues and dealt with them.

The driver of the car returned for her senior year and graduated in good standing. She had no major incidents again.

One boy who withdrew petitioned to come back, worked hard to deal with his issues, and had good support from his parents. They were realistic about the risks, knew the school was the best option, and were willing to take the chance for their son. The school administration accepted him under strict conditions. Sadly, it didn't work out, and they had to recognize his dismissal when he made another major mistake the next fall.

The last boy did not even attempt to return.

The law played its role, justice was served, and I did not have to deal with lawyers.

Our legal system is based on an adversarial model. There is prosecution and defense—with lawyers on both sides; often win versus lose with winner take all; interests of the defendant versus interests of the society, which also represents the victim. It can be simple; it usually is not. Often the process is simplified by plea bargaining, and it can be relatively smooth if there is truthfulness from the beginning. Situation A happens, consequence B results. We move on. That even happens once in a while. It would not make for gripping television, an exciting movie, or a good novel. We would like life to be clear and simple but we love our imagination to run wild for our entertainment.

When I was a boy I thought anyone could grow up to be President and that was something to strive for. Of course, I knew nothing of power, of politics, of the burdens of responsibility, but the ideal was something to strive for. I left that dream behind and eventually found what I liked to do. Working in the same place for 33 years makes me something of an anachronism, but that does not mean I have not been interested in what is happening elsewhere. I have not rekindled any desire to be President, but I more fully appreciate what the job means.

As a history teacher and someone who follows the daily news religiously, I am a fan of *West Wing*. There again there are some ethical dilemmas, this time in the context of national and international situations rather than in schools or cities. There is also the issue of the President of the United States as the single representative of the nation while at the same time having a personal life; but sometimes the roles conflict. As in the situation of Bill Clinton and some of the poor decisions in his personal life, the boundary line of what is personal and what is political is not always clear. Thus we have the anomaly of a popular President contemned by a majority of Americans. The American public could see, although they were not pleased by it, the distinction between what was important for the man as President and what was important for the man as husband and father. The ethical dilemma in *West Wing* is a medical condition, not disclosed and arguably hidden by the President and his advisers. What does the public have a right to know?

The main character in *West Wing* not only is President, father of three daughters, husband to a prominent surgeon, son of a feisty father, and prep school graduate; he is also a Pulitzer prize winning economist, literary master, biblical expert, chess player, enologist, raconteur, and dispenser of assorted factoids, decisive judgment and wisdom. He is the sort of person a Dean would aspire to emulate. Except, perhaps, for the economics.

This television program blends into my chapter on politics, which is the intent of the show itself. The distinction between decision-making and the process by which the decision is reached is often far more complex than we on the outside can understand or perhaps even want to know. I certainly know that dilemma as Dean, and seeing some of our student leaders grapple with the issues that confront them is instructive for both them and me as we search for solutions to problems.

Sometimes the student leader—President of the Student Council, editor of the newspaper, proctor in a dorm—knows more about a disciplinary situation than he or she is comfortable with. It is analogous to the lawyer-client privilege, but more commonly with the peer-adult dichotomy. The conflict is disturbing to students; they know they are students rather than adults, and that what is "right" in protecting students can conflict with what is "right" according to the rules of the school.

The President of the Student Council is not like the President of the United States. The former has no power to make decisions, but he or she does have responsibility to the institution. Part of that responsibility is to hold the high moral ground in public, to be somewhat of an occupant of the bully pulpit. Yet that means that the student Presidents should be above criticism; they are increasingly aware of the possibility of the hypocrisy they are charged to expose. But if they are popular enough to get elected to some high office, it means that they know well many students—their peers. Knowledge can be a dangerous power. In West Wing we sometimes see the characters struggling with what they do not want to know.

In the 2001-2002 school year we have seen a new program called *The Agency*. Coincidentally with 9/11 we have the resurrection of the CIA as a necessity in preventing evil from triumphing. It's an exciting show, full of James Bond kinds of gadgets and heroism, reminiscent also of Mr. Phelps and *Mission Impossible*, for those of us slightly older. It also has the complexity of the law shows in that there is underlying purpose of elevating the agency to a respectable status after several decades of negative perception. 9/11 reinforced the need for intelligence gathering and preventive action.

We debate the preventive action constantly. Should we intervene before the student hurts self or community? Should we break the rules or circumvent them in the interests of the greater good? The rules were made after the community was created, not before, so the idea that there is a universal truth means that it must be discovered, not created.

I do not like breaking the rules, but I have done so. I have done a room search without someone else present, not as a thorough investigation but to confirm the presence of a weapon or drugs someone has reported to me. I do not like room searches in general, but if there is immediate cause—under the influence, possession, or evidence like smell that suggests illegal activity—then the immediate room search is not a problem. However, I think it sends a disturbing message to the community when room searches result from somebody else's word or due to rumor.

What about rights? Especially with students who are studying some kind of law-related issue, the discussion of rights is always worth a good debate, if not a confrontation. But there are a variety of levels of rights. There are human rights, there are civil rights, there are contractual rights. There are also laws, and there are rules. Possession of alcohol for someone under 21 is against the law so it is also against the rules. Wearing a hat in the dining commons is against the rules but not against the law.

Searching a room that the school owns by school officials is within the rules; search by the police needs a warrant.

When students enroll in the school they and their parents sign a contract in which they acknowledge the rules of the school as they appear in the Student Handbook:

> We agree that the School retains the right to deny registration or access to program services, including classroom instruction, unless tuition and fee payments are current, required health records have been submitted in accordance with School procedures, and the student remains in good standing academically and socially (please refer to the guidelines set forth in the Course of Studies Booklet and Student Handbook). Furthermore, we agree that the School may refuse to allow the Student to take examinations and may withhold grades and transcripts in the event that any monies due to the School have not been paid in full.

Part of my job is to enforce the rules of the Handbook, but I also have to be part of the bigger picture for both the school and the individual. Would I lie to get something? I do not lie to entrap students. I am sure someone may find some exception to that over my career, but that is what I believe. I might lie to prevent some activity that would be harmful to someone. I have a hard time doing that, and I prefer to deflect inquiries by not telling the whole truth. If someone asked me if a particular individual had "ratted" on him, I would say it was not the person's business who told me what. However, I do not want to be in the situation where not denying a particular piece of information seems like confirmation.

There is also the reality that a person is not formally an adult until the age of eighteen. And for the rules, as opposed to the law, any students, eighteen or nineteen or on occasion even twenty, have to comply. If they buy cigarettes in the town they are breaking the rule of possession, even though they are not breaking the law. There is a growing trend, although certainly not dominant in much of American society, that the adults—parents and school personnel in my school—are the final decision-makers, not the student under eighteen. And sometimes that is a difficult lesson for the adults after we have given so much responsibility for decision-making to teenagers. Nevertheless, I think we are beginning to have more concerted action between the parents and the school personnel for that process. We agree that that the adults in the process must have greater accountability for our youth.

I watched a program of *Crossing Jordan* where an athlete died because he had an arrhythmic heartbeat but told his mother he was going to play basketball anyway. She allowed him, because it was his decision. The medical examiner then decided that he would tell his own daughter she could not go away for a getaway weekend to "chill" after the death of this boy, who was her friend. He and his wife, separated but perhaps on the verge of getting back together, now decided to act in concert and no longer allow the teenage daughter to play one off against the other. The theme was that the adults were in charge until the child was eighteen, and they would make the decisions until then. It took the immediacy of a death to encourage the parent to take charge, to exercise the responsibility that was his as a parent.

In my school over the last decade, the adults have gradually been taking more initiative, setting not only parameters of the rules but enforcing them as well. This has not gone on without opposition and will continue to require dialog, but the goal is to protect the students as best we can without taking away all the risks. In this case, I think the television culture is catching up with at least our own school culture.

Not only do teenagers need boundaries, clear ones that are both reasonable and justifiable, but teenagers want them, perhaps not openly or at the moment gratefully, but they want them. And I will stand on the fact that I am an adult and a teenager is not and that there is a difference, and a difference we need to keep in front of us.

Students also want to be able to challenge the boundaries and move them if that is the right action. A *Boston Public* show about the same time took on the topic of the word "nigger" and the book by the same title. The principal, who was black, told the teacher, who was white, to desist from further discussion of the "nigger" issue in his classroom. He reluctantly acceded, but his students pushed him to allow further discussion. The end result was the black principal taking over the class and moderating the discussion, bowing to the pressure of the students not to fire the teacher and the pressure of the teacher not to drop the discussion.

I feel like I have grown away from the escapist humor of *Seinfeld* and *Frasier*, and maybe that is simply the reflection of what I am doing this year. Yet I think these evening shows are also expanding on the problems that are confronting us as a society and challenging everyone to take on the topics that have always been there but have been glossed over.

I am not a fan of television for kids except for legitimate entertainment and education. By that I mean TV watching is a conscious choice rather than a passive reaction to a lack of energy to do anything else. Television often promotes dehumanization, crass materialism, desensitization, violence, sexism, racism and obesity to name a few of the vices I object to. But I have moved from begrudging TV its positive moments to applauding outright the instructive and thought-provoking programming of the shows I have mentioned. While not all of the episodes were equally worthwhile, I have learned something from all of them.

THE TECHNOLOGY CHALLENGE

The challenges of technology as it affects kids and as they utilize it makes me think of the dog track, the greyhounds racing around the track trying to catch a mechanical rabbit that is always just ahead of them. The dogs cover a lot of ground quickly but never catch the rabbit.

Most of the adults in the community know that the students are well ahead of us in the technology area, and we come to rely on a few experts among us as well as some sympathetic allies in the student body. Some schools now have larger technology staffs than academic departments within the school. The bureaucracy of schools has grown tremendously over the last couple of decades, and the teaching staff has plenty of fodder for their faculty room, lunchroom, and faculty office discussions. Money and time have been noticeably spent on business offices, development offices, technology departments, admissions offices and communications offices at a far greater pace than on teaching faculty.

I remember when I was a sophomore at this same school radios were allowed for the first time. What a distraction they must have appeared to be to the faculty at that time. Nevertheless, we all survived, and if any of us did not go to college it was not because of radios.

I am not sure the same could be said about the technology of the 21st century. We went from radios to turntables, to walkmans, to computers. We added telephones for everyone; now everyone seems to have cell phones. VCRs themselves are to be outmoded soon with DVDs and the pervasive influence of the Internet. I hesitate to dream about the next inventions that will hit us, but invention has become the mother of necessity.

For some students who make it through our rigorous program, the next level is even more challenging, not because of the academic demands but rather because of the lack of monitoring of the influences. While we emphasize the importance of independence in student thinking and, to a relatively large degree in acting, we admit to ourselves as adults and to them as teenagers that they are not free, that they are not yet fully prepared for the challenges ahead, and that we as the school, the village elders, still have our rules that we think are best. We try to exercise our authority without being authoritarian, making adjustments to new technology as we think appropriate. Most of the time we are re-acting; we can hardly be ahead of the curve.

Certainly one of the major technological changes that has come about while I have been Dean has been the introduction of a telephone for every boarding student, with a voice mail system for messages that also includes the commuting students as part of the system. Anyone can access messages from any telephone, but at least during the school day the boarding students are more accustomed to checking; they have a little red light on the telephone in their room indicating they have a message. They check regularly, eagerly anticipating some important communication—at least at first.

One small glitch in the wonderful new communication system for the Dean's Office was that students would learn not to retrieve their messages if they did not want them. We could deal with the passive aggressive nature of their responses to *our* communications, but when they did not respond to their parents' entreaties we would get additional calls to our office to track down the offending youth and make him or her call home. The same was true of the commuters; they simply did not bother to check their messages and we would have to continue to play the role of messenger. The proliferation of cell phones has compounded the communication problem.

We tried to anticipate as best we could the problems as well as the advantages of the new telephone system; other schools had already been at this and had experience that we could build on.

The advantages include students not having to share the single pay phone in the dorm; the privacy of conversation in the room; the ability to leave and retrieve messages.

The system includes timers so that we can turn the telephones off during the mandatory evening study hall and after the time students are to be in their own rooms for the night. The system automatically goes back on 6:30 AM and any messages would be waiting. We also leave common room phones on for emergencies, and anyone can access the 911 system at any time from any phone.

The system also includes a tracking ability so that we can monitor which phones are being used and to some degree what numbers are being called to and from. We found we did not have the physical capacity to record all the calls, but some information was better than none. Complaints about monitoring have been almost non-existent.

One of our initial concerns was harassment. We know that kids like to vent their feelings over the phone, and they do have the capacity to be mean and hurtful. They can also be threatening. A few students were foolish enough to leave messages on other students' phones that were not appropriate. These situations were easily addressed. The more difficult were annoying phone calls or unwanted phone calls. At least we can track those and insist they cease on pain of formal punishment. I would even write up "contracts" between students that threatened Probation if they used any kind of harassing communication after they had been told to stop.

A technological glitch we found we had to address early was access to outside lines. As most everyone does, we used the nine to connect to the outside line. The problem for us was that we make many international calls, both from administrative offices and student rooms. And fingers occasionally were too light on the zero; thus, we dialed 911. The local constabulary became frustrated. The last straw was when the Dean himself missed the zero. We changed from the nine to the eight for outside calls and have resolved that problem.

A second problem with 911 is that the calls are only identified from the trunk lines, which means that the individual telephone extensions are not identified. When I called from my office, had I hung up they would have known that it was only the school line rather than me in particular. We have to train our students that if they use 911, they have to stay on the phone and clearly identify where they are. "Come quick. My room is on fire" followed by a hang-up is not fully helpful

Inquisitive students quickly discovered a third glitch. They learned that the connection to another party was not severed when the phone lines were shut off by the computer-controlled system. The phone had to be hung up. So students talking with each other when the system turned off could keep the line open all night if they wanted. Dorm parents and student proctors had to hone their sleuthing skills because students did not simply keep talking; they devised ways to make it appear that the phone was hung up until their rooms had had the final check. One device was the toothpaste cap placed in a neat fit over the telephone hookflash. The hookflash did not get depressed, the connection was still live, and the game was on.

While as adults we did not lose a great deal of sleep over this transgression, the above did point out that technology can always be humanly manipulated. And the adults in education are not always at the cutting edge; sometimes their students are! As in other areas of school life, worrying over the toothpaste cap caper is better than worrying over illicit drug use, presuming the latter is part of our routine awareness rather than the focus of current crisis.

The switches to set the timers are another checkpoint in our telephone technology. We decided to put them in my office, that the Dean should be Control in the system. Because we have classes on alternate Saturdays, we have evening study halls from 8-10 on some Fridays and not others. The timers can be programmed for a weekly cycle, but on weeks when the Friday routine changes, the hours for that day have to be reset manually. The same situation occurs on the two weekends when we change the clocks for the onset or end of Daylight Savings Time. While the consequences of not having made the correct adjustments are no more than annoying, they are one other little detail to be factored into the duties of the Dean. Students seem careful not to tell us if the phones are on when they should not be, but they are quick to note the opposite.

Between the introduction of telephones for everyone and the pervasive cell phone explosion, came a short period when we wrestled over the cordless phone issue. We decreed that cordless phones attached to our system were not allowed, mostly because their use interfered with other phones on the campus. We did have a couple of embarrassing situations where students were listening into faculty member conversations that were meant to be strictly private.

Cell phones have proliferated in the last several years, first from our Asian students who seemed to be on the technological cusp, ahead of our American students. These phones were particularly helpful for those students in communicating with their parents, whose time zones were twelve-fourteen hours different from ours. But then they began to be used for more mundane purposes. We debated what to do, with some people wanting to outlaw and confiscate them, others simply wanting to regulate how they were used. We decided to allow them, but the students had to abide by the same rules governing our school phones; i.e., not during study hall or after hours, unless they had permission.

Now, many students have cell phones. Our commuters use them all the time because the phones obviate the need to use voice mail, especially when a parent wants to communicate. Of course, that is now not the most obvious reason students are using the phone. We do not allow our students to use them in class, assemblies, or in other places where they would be disruptive to normal routine. Cell phone records can be a good resource for parents to know how much time students are spending chatting, when they are chatting, and whether the use of the phone is interfering with other uses of time. Whether we have the technology is not so important as to how we use it.

Individual telephones for each boarding student have been overwhelmingly a positive influence for us as a school. More communication is better than less, and even though there has been a rise in inappropriate communication, it has been dwarfed by the positive outcomes.

Computer technology is the other major influence that has blossomed over the last decade. Schools try to understand how to utilize it in the educational setting; individuals try to make it a valuable part of their lives; Deans try to anticipate and deal with all the negatives. Actually, I give way too much credit to Deans because by and large we are not technocrats.

As we did with telephones, we made available access for every boarding student to have a port to hook up a computer to our own server. Prior to that we used the phone lines, and we were almost instantly overwhelmed with use. People could not access the phones because so many were on-line. Then we purchased our own server with a high-speed connection and separated the computers from the telephones. Every student has an email account, and certainly one challenge has been to get people to use it. We added every member of the community to the email access, created special sections for different sectors of the community, installed computers throughout the campus, and informed students on a regular basis that we wanted them to use the system; all this in addition to teaching Romeo and Juliet and Algebra II.

As with the telephones, almost instant computer and Internet access enhanced communication, that goddess of improvement to all human growth. Of course, communication like technology depends on the hands that are using it, and with the good came the not so good.

As with the telephones, we put a timer on the accessibility to the computers connected to our server; the computers automatically shut down at 12:00 AM during the week and 12:30 AM on weekends, coming back on-line at 6:30 AM. Unlike the phone system, which requires disconnection, the computers do not. When the system shuts down, all the connections automatically are disconnected. Students can still use the computers for word processing or accessing whatever else might be on their own sets, but they cannot communicate with other computers.

The term IM eased into my lexicon, although students knew

much more about it several years ago than I know now, but IM stands for Instant Messaging, essentially talking in conversation through the computer: I write a sentence, you respond, and back and forth we go. It's a telephone without interruption; it can get a whole sentence in without being cut off. Students wanted this feature immediately, and we struggled to both give the access and to oversee that it was not abused.

Abuse can take several forms, such as overuse, inappropriate use, and even non-use. Because we decided not to turn off the computers during our study period—this was to give access to research on the Internet and other positive uses of the technology—we made a rule that students could not use IM during the 8-10 PM study hall period and could not play games, listen or view sports or entertainment, etc. Our attempts to control computer use are a little bit like building a sand castle on the beach with the incoming tide, but the statement at least made us feel good about trying to slow the distracting element of computers. Our experience has also taught us that many students with academic difficulties or less than expected achievements were overusing the computer, especially for IM or chatting. Again we could monitor how the system was being used, and if a student were spending an inordinate amount of time in chat rooms or otherwise, it would give us an opportunity to intervene. The computer communication can be similar to any other kind of addiction: the individual is overwhelmed by the addictive behavior, which controls the individual rather than the other way around.

When the students go off to college they have found a wonderful way to keep in touch with their old friends as well as new ones, but excessive computer use has become an important factor in college dropout rates. Too much time on the Internet has replaced poker games, bridge sessions and other face-to-face activities that may have been cause for failures in college, or perhaps even boarding school.

Perhaps one small factor in our battle against this kind of failure has been our specific attention to consequences for missed commitments. If a student stayed up late on the computer playing games then that student may have difficulty getting up in the morning, sometimes missing classes. It took us a while to get a good system in place for holding students accountable for their absences, but now we feel comfortable with what we do. There is a balance between what we do as adults, or administrators in an institution, and what individual responsibility lies with the student. We shut off the Internet, but we do not "force" students to go to bed. If they want to stay up late, then they will have to face up to whatever negative consequences may fall their way. We are neither authoritarian nor completely individualistic. We are comfortable with the shared responsibility, knowing that there will always be something imperfect.

Another problem we faced was the creation of a Web site, which used the school's name but was sponsored by an individual student. The student wanted to create a forum whereby students could voice their concerns and opinions outside the jurisdiction of the school. The school newspaper still had too much connection to the institution because it had a faculty adviser and therefore was not completely "free". Publication schedules also meant there was a delay between an important issue and the need to discuss it. The Internet provided that means of instant discussion. Unfortunately, it also provided anonymity. What people will do outside the scrutiny of anyone else runs a gamut that includes vicious commentary as well as libelous, salacious, and generally unattractive material.

The Webmaster—the facilitator of this site—lost control of what was being put on the site. As the readership expanded, it eventually included adults in the community, both those at the school and parents who were at home. It took us a few days to get the site off the network and hold the individual accountable for creating the website and for what appeared there, despite the fact that that he himself was not guilty of the most offensive material that was actually being posted. We also could not "prove" who was saying the most vicious of the material, but we did manage to have the student close the site. Several students faced a variety of penalties, but there was pain that lingered for several months.

Eventually, the person who was probably the chief offender of the worst contributions to the site left the school at the end of the year, only a couple of weeks away. It was not a great way to end the school year.

As with the issue of homophobia, the ability to hide behind a cloak—the image of a white hooded robe comes to mind—is dangerous. Free speech does not include harassment, slander or libel. Opinions are legitimate to hold, but the holder must be willing to stand by them—openly. Actions taken based on those opinions may not be legal; we hope to educate about opinions, we are compelled to act by behaviors.

The computer has spawned several other technological advances; some are improvements, some are distractions. Some of the improvements also have the potential for negative effects if they are used poorly. An example is the research power of the Internet. Students do not have to leave their rooms to get material to write papers. They do not have to go to the library to do research; they can do it on-line.

There is a convenience to staying in one place with instant access to material, but it also a temptation for abuse. We can simply copy chunks of material from the computer—generated documents. Then it is an easy temptation to neglect to give credit to the original source. We call that plagiarism. It is a major offense in the academic community, one of our major rules. We do make a qualification to recognize the indiscretion of youth: for a ninth or tenth grade student the first offense for plagiarism is a notification plus the academic zero. Such plagiarism does not get Probation until the second offense. When students have reached the mature age of the eleventh grade, we expect a clearer understanding of right from wrong and do not have a grace period; Probation occurs on the first offense.

We have recently seen well-known and highly respected writers and professional historians get caught up in the ease of access to other people's words. Sometimes they are deliberately copying; sometimes they are just lazy. The result is illegal regardless of the motive, but there are certainly shades of guilt Acronyms and abbreviations using the first letter of each word in a group have become a mainstay of our language. Perhaps they emerged full force with the New Deal of Franklin Roosevelt beginning in 1933, even though the word acronym did not appear until 1943. Abbreviations by first letter began at the end of the previous century. We remember the alphabet soup agencies that were created in the 1930's—AAA, CCC, NRA—rather than the names. Now we see acronyms daily.

One I use is CASE. I go to conferences from time to time to learn and share. Somebody said that CASE was something we should utilize as teachers to expand our knowledge and understanding: Copy And Steal Everything. Clearly this was meant in a pedagogical sense; teachers know that copying is cheating or plagiarism. The word steal bothered me so I modified the acronym to mean "share" instead of "steal". If we share what we know the recipients will grow. The sages among us do not keep their wisdom to themselves.

In the pedagogical sense the Internet has great possibilities. Nevertheless, we must appreciate the dangers. The easy access has spawned companies and individuals who will sell other people's works to buyers. In education, we see research or term papers for sale on any topic and on any level someone may want. While the Academic Dean could certainly provide me with plenty of examples, I have seen some in my own classes and have had to deal with some through the Dean's Office where Probation was going to jeopardize a student's position in the school. We have in fact expelled students for plagiarizing, and the consequences of that behavior have severe repercussions for the next level of education. Colleges are much more understanding of behavioral transgressions like drugs, alcohol, and sneaking out of the dorm than they are of academic integrity issues. Breaking the law with a six pack of beer is not seen as an indictment of character; cheating and plagiarism are.

Students do not generally understand that their teachers recognize their personal writing styles, including the vocabulary that they use. A sudden and dramatic change is an obvious transgression. It is sad watching a student tell us that he knows what the word "trepidation" means and how it fits into the context of the sentence. We all would rather see a quick admission of guilt and move on with the appropriate penalties, but it does not always work that way.

What a tangled web we weave. Shakespeare . . . somewhere. I am deliberately being lazy here because every day we are using others' words and phrases, and I think that fits into the CASE scenario. Copying the whole scene from that Shakespeare play without acknowledging it would be plagiarism.

Another technological innovation that is blossoming is the DVD—Digital Video Display. The VCR, like the copying machine, came earlier and had wonderful applications for classroom use. The DVD is a more advanced version and is now connected to the computer. Students can watch movies in the comfort of their own rooms. VCR's needed televisions, and our students are not allowed to have personal televisions. We did install them in a common room in every dormitory, recognizing that our society is overwhelmed with technology and the images it produces. We all know that we would be better off reading a book like Abraham Lincoln did, but I am afraid the marketplace has a strong hold on us. Which boarding school would the student applicant choose: the one with no televisions and VCR's or the one that has them? Even the parents would weigh in with the reality of the choice. After all, parents have been struggling the last several decades with whose house the children want to visit. Is it the quality of the cookies, the dynamism of the supervising parent, the accessibility of technological toys?

It is incumbent upon us to consider the implications of the changes produced by technology. Being a Luddite—referring to a group of 19th century radicals who tried to destroy machinery because it was changing their way of life—is not going to be effective. Cell phones, computers, the Internet, DVD's and other soon-to-be-introduced changes are here. We need to use them without them using us; no mean feat.

Other technological changes are not appropriate in our educational and social village. I have talked about guns in a different place. Another example is the use of laser lights. They are annoying, hard to detect, and potentially dangerous. While I was in the process of confiscating this small, battery-powered bullet-sized device a couple of years ago, there was concurrently a court case in the next city addressing the issue. Someone from a window was lighting up a pedestrian on the sidewalk with a laser beam. The beamer was accused of assault and was successfully prosecuted.

I rarely see weapons, but I know of certain kinds of knives, chukkas, brass knuckles and other dangerous items that are illegal in the state. I have confiscated a few, seen other examples at the local police station, and have no tolerance for their presence in our community. Every knife is a potential weapon, but that is not the purpose of a bread knife, Swiss army knife, or a steak knife. However, since 9/11 we are all a little more wary.

We are not aware of all the activities our teenagers are up to, and they do need some space to grow, to make mistakes, to learn consequences and responsibilities. But we have to recognize our own ignorance and naiveté.

Parents and teachers realize their kids know more about technology than the adults. The adults then sometimes assume that the children will use the technology appropriately. Adults know more about the negative effects of drugs, alcohol, pornography, hatred, and outright meanness. It is incumbent upon parents to monitor the activities of their children, not only as they behave but as they use technology. I know this is a major challenge.

Although students in the boarding school can hide behind doors, just as they can do in their own homes, the Internet access is in many cases more tightly controlled here than it is in the home. Many parents have given their children their own phone lines and Internet connections; the children are independent and unmonitored. The monitoring is just one more burden that many parents do not take on, for any of a number of reasons. They need to take it on.

CASUALTIES

One of the first books I read after I became Dean was *Casualties of Privilege*, a devastatingly critical analysis of what went on within the boundaries of the elite prep schools. It was a series of essays by former students, edited by Louis Crosier, outlining the inside workings from the student perspective. Privilege, in the form of wealth and opportunity to go to high-powered college preparatory secondary schools, did not exempt students from either being victims of a variety of physical and emotional abuses or perpetrators of them. The privileged did, though, often get special treatment as either victims or perpetrators.

I also remember reading Jonathan Kozol's book, *Death at an Early Age*, when it came out. I was in graduate school, studying history over thirty years ago. Potential subtitles for that depressing look at our educational system as it affected our least privileged students certainly could include the word Casualties. Watching Boston Public made me reflect on what the schools were like in Boston nearly 40 years earlier when Jonathan Kozol began his teaching.

Casualties can be permanent losses or temporary losses, disasters or victims. For some there is another chance. Kozol described many who never had a first chance, never mind a second one. They may still be suffering from their experiences, but they were only damaged, not destroyed.

In 1970 a book about a boarding school cracked the shell of life on the inside of such a school. The author, a graduate of the school itself some fifteen years earlier, asked the Head if he could return and stay for a couple of months at the beginning of the 1967-68 school year. He stayed through the spring because it was becoming such a tumultuous year, tumultuous both for the school and the country.

Unlike Crosier, who utilized former students, Peter Prescott in *A World of Our Own* observed the life of the school while in its midst, listening to students, faculty and administrators. The Head was a particularly prominent player, and the autocratic nature of most boarding schools made them ripe for the changes that were about to befall them, Prescott's no less than my own. While the particular story about my own school is for someone else to tell, autocracy and single sex education were casualties of that era. Most would feel that those were necessary casualties if schools were going to be better.

Interestingly enough, that school—a prestigious one—did not suffer much from the exposure, nor did it suffer from a drug-running scandal by a student nearly twenty-years later. In fact, the latter resulted in increased interest in the school, partly perhaps because of name recognition, partly perhaps because they had a problem and they dealt with it. The era of denial and circling the wagons in defense of privilege was, for the most part, over. Nevertheless, privilege remains.

Protection of our own, whether it is the family, the village, the school, or our personal lives, still exerts a powerful pressure. It can be a healthy or destructive protection, and once again judgment and opinion play a role. My protectiveness is probably normal. I have erred on both sides of the issue; sometimes I have divulged information I should not have, sometimes the reverse. Each situation presents something unique.

Many schools—my own included—now have a Communications office and director. I have not had the press call me yet, for which I am thankful, but if they do, I can defer to the Communications Director. Schools have added this specialization along with many others, and for the most part having a specialist for outside communication is probably more positive than negative. We cannot be in our own world without contact or inquiry from the outside, and while it somehow seems anomalous that we need communication experts for schools—we do.

Neither privilege nor poverty precludes neglect. Kids of all ages and background can suffer. The privileged, however, have a much greater opportunity to recover. There is an enduring image, and even one that is sometimes true, of troubled kids or unloved kids being sent away to boarding schools to get reformed as well as educated. Perhaps there is an unspoken hope that in some way they will also get loved. Love takes many forms. In the context of simply having someone care enough about a child to attend to the casualties inflicted, to try to perform whatever healing needs to be done, love is a resource that can make a school better than just an institution for learning.

When any of us enters a new village we quickly perceive the sense of welcome or rejection, of friendliness or wariness. Good schools anywhere should not be triaging new members as though they were already casualties; however, that is exactly what some schools are created for. And they are not just boarding schools. We now have public schools whose purpose is to be a place where all those casualties of our society that cannot fit into mainstream education can get attention and some skills to enable them to at least survive if not thrive in the community. We have even heard discussion about some public schools taking on a boarding population for the school week to ensure that students have a healthy and safe environment at least for the period of time they are attending school. The practicalities of that idea—facilities, personnel, governance—has made any implementation almost impossible.

The casualties that do arrive at established boarding schools are not so obvious at first, because they would not be admitted if they were indeed so troubled that they would not fit. Many would like to attend but are not able to for reasons of finances, of past performance, of unresolved issues. We are able to make that assessment before they even arrive. The ones that attend are indeed privileged. However, privilege has the power to cover hidden wounds with clever dressing.

The Dean is certainly not the person who is charged with healing casualties, but the Dean can certainly be one of the people who helps to identify students who need help. The Dean is also not the person designated to spread love throughout the school and ensure that every student is carefully attended to. Love emanates from individual people, not from institutions. We often talk about our school as being a warm and friendly place, while also being a place of academic rigor. If it is so, it is because the people in it are warm and friendly yet demanding of their students. There is nothing about the geography of a place, about the credentials of its members, or about the programs it offers that ensures warmth and care. These qualities need to be nurtured by the people there.

Reputations and images evolve, they do not change overnight. If an institution or a village has been known in a particular way, a sweeping change by a new Head or by a new statement of philosophy is not going to change the reputation. If an institution is considered "good" by certain standards it is called prestigious; some schools have prestige, most do not. The prestige indeed can mean good, or it can simply be a cover. My school does not bask in prestige; philosophically, I do not think we would want it, but we would like the benefits that accrue to prestige without the baggage that can accompany it. We could not be a place that allowed casualties to go unattended. That is not to say there are institutions that do, but there can be a deniability factor that pervades a place. I doubt that the term Peyton Place means much to anyone now, but in the 1950's and 1960's it had that ring to it: there was much beneath the surface that the people in it did not want the outside to know about. Novelists and chroniclers have studied this phenomenon for as long as they have been recording. Critical self-examination, without the angst of being a guilt-ridden group, produces a healthier product as well as a better place. That applies to the industrial world, the social world, and the educational world.

There are none so blind as those who will not see. We all practice denial once in a while, some of it is born out of simple optimism, some of it from naiveté, all of it with a hope that the situation will get better. I, personally, am not very good at what has been termed "tough love." I understand it, appreciate those that can do it well, see its value in some cases. It just is not my style. I am more inclined to try another, softer approach; tough love at my school essentially means expulsion—we call it

Dismissal—and that means that we can no longer work with the student. Dismissal is sometimes the appropriate response, and I am supportive of that in some cases, perhaps not in as many as some others might, but in fact more than some of my teaching colleagues. I have more difficulty with being the authority that says that the person must go. I work hard to get the student and the parents to make that decision. And sometimes they won't. They want someone else to take the responsibility. Then there is someone to blame. Usually it is the parents who do not want to accept the decision that the student must be expelled. Rarely is the child of that set of parents, or individual parent, not already a casualty. We have not had the time or the resources, if they exist at all, to heal what has been hurting for a long time.

Although this scene from *Peyton Place* is not a central part of the plot, it is telling about a parental relationship with both a son and a school:

> As the years passed, Leslie continued to "boss" his mills and his town, but he did not "boss" his son. This, too, was of his own choosing. It pleased him when he saw reflected in Rodney the traits which were his.
>
> "Got gumption, that kid has," Leslie often said. "There's not a trace of the weak-kneed Fullers in him."
>
> In this, Leslie Harrington was badly mistaken, for Rodney was weak in the terrible, final way in which only those who are protected and surrounded by powerful externals are weak. Rodney never had to be strong, for strength was all around him, readymade to protect and shield him. Nor was Rodney driven by a compulsion to succeed as was his father. True, he liked to win well enough, but not to the extent that he would fight and struggle to win, especially if his opponents happened to be his physical match. Before he was ten years old, Rodney knew that there was nothing worth winning that involved effort, for without effort he could win anything he wanted from his father. He had merely to ask or, later, to hold out his hand, and whatever he

wanted was his. Yet Rodney was not a fool. He knew that it
was politic for him to please his father whenever he could,
especially when it involved no sacrifice on his part. Thus,
when he had been younger and his father had wanted him
to associate with "nice" 'children, Rodney had done so, It
made no difference to him. He could be King anywhere.
And later, when his father had wanted him to go to New
Hampton, Rodney had gone willingly. He hated school
anyway, so it did not matter to him where he went. When
he was expelled, he had not been afraid to come home and
face his father.

"I got bounced, Dad," he said.

"'What the hell for?"

"Too much drinking and girling, I guess."

"Well, for Christ's sake!"

Leslie had gone at once to the headmaster at New
Hampton and told him what he thought of a school that
tried to prevent a youngster from sowing a few wild oats.

'I'm paying you to teach him a few academic courses,"
Leslie had shouted, "not to worry about what he does with
his free time. I'll worry about that."

(p. 206-7)

Even in the 1939 scene that this represents, there is an attitude
that occasionally rears its unattractive head in the 21st century.
More likely, the criticism at this later time would center on the
school's lack of responsibility for the free time where the student
has had difficulty with the social rules of the school.

There are schools that are specifically designed to correct
imbalances that have devastated a student and the family. We refer
to them as therapeutic schools. They are tough, demanding, and
expensive. They are also, like any school, a temporary place, an
institution designed to help adolescents get to another place where
they will continue to be, or perhaps become, successful. Many of
them have a strong outdoor education component. They all stress
counseling. If we think a graduate of such a program is ready for

our kind of school, we will accept the applicant; some have done very well, some have not.

I went to a conference once where a director of such a school was extolling the success of my school because of the integration of one of their graduates into our program. He did not know I was in the audience so the story told was not for my benefit. Nevertheless, the girl he was referring to was indeed a success (she was a junior), and part of the reason he thought she had succeeded was that she was accepted by her peers for who she was and was not judged by where she had been. In the opening meetings in the dorm, she had told her story, and her dorm mates had implicitly accepted her without critical judgment. They had listened, even admired her courage in revealing her difficulties, and were willing to judge her on her behavior as to who she was at that point rather than on what her background had been.

She went on to become a proctor as a senior, but in the second semester of her senior year she was discovered with beer in her refrigerator. She said she did not know who had put it there, but she took the consequences anyway. What she did not know was that I had seen a photograph of her at a birthday party of a classmate's earlier in the winter. A whole group of students had signed out to this person's house for a gala 18th birthday celebration and one of her friends had taken pictures. One photo included her drinking beer; another showed a keg.

I questioned a number of people about the party, without revealing that I had seen pictures. There was denial across the board, including the parents hosting the party. Almost everyone had signed out correctly. There was an exception that we struggled with, someone who signed out to a day student's home and then went with the day student across state lines to this party without parental knowledge or consent. The responsibility for what occurred at the party, however, lay with the host parents. They, sadly but expectedly, stonewalled and denied knowledge of any drinking, and certainly knowledge of any keg. No school consequences resulted from that party

Weeks later, though, the girl who was suspended had to

confront her parents, who were very supportive of our actions, deal with her suspension and loss of proctorship, and finish the year successfully. She did all that and went on to a well-respected small liberal arts college. There was enough structure, support, follow-up, and oversight that she had a successful career at our school.

Perhaps we enabled her. She dropped out of college in her freshman year, a casualty of privilege? Perhaps she was a casualty of not enough support.

Other students coming from those kinds of therapeutic schools have had their share of success and failure. Those schools work very hard to reintegrate students back into the mainstream. Often there has been drug and alcohol abuse and family dysfunction that are addressed by people specifically trained for these issues. Intense work by the teaching staff, the residential staff, and the psychologists can get these kids through their difficult teenage years and back on to a track where they will become successful adults. Nevertheless, I assume that those students that leave that extremely supportive environment will need more attention at our school than the average student.

While my school offers a strong program to help kids get through the normal teenage difficulties, we are not a therapeutic school. Some students need that additional outside support and receive it, but sometimes that is not enough.

The casualties from drug and alcohol use I address in other chapters, but sometimes there are physical casualties that are the normal part of life. These often have some other ramifications. I have learned to look for signs after I have seen a casualty.

One area that stands out for me is the student athlete who has to be sidelined because of an injury or illness. Our school requires participation in sports—or in a designated and acceptable alternative program—every season. There are three seasons during the school year. For some students this activity is vital to their success. It is part of their self-esteem. They may even hope for participation in a top-level collegiate athletic program. When they cannot play or practice they can become depressed. They may then self-medicate with drugs or alcohol. They may behave inappropriately. Our school is able to deal with such individuals more readily, but the public school system has fewer resources.

The budget cuts in the public school systems around the country have had a severe impact on school programs. Programs like athletics, arts, foreign language, and extra-curricular activities are the ones eliminated. The consequences of those cuts have long-term implications for the students who need those opportunities for their energy and their growth. But if growth is going to be measured only in its material value, the spiritual/moral/aesthetic consequences for our society in the long term are not especially healthy.

Everything has a cost, usually a financial one but often a qualitative one. If we are going to pay our teachers good salaries, if we are going to have good facilities, if we are going to educate everyone regardless of their needs, we will have to spend more money. That means raising more money, read taxes, or cutting costs. Long term investment is not always a strong point in our capitalist, independence oriented, individualistic society. The attitude of "I am willing to do my share, but I see no need to spoil these kids with all these unnecessary extras" leaves little choice for the school committees and administrators. They choose to boost salaries of the core teachers, make sure the facilities are safe and utile, and invest in the most up-to-date technology. The other programs will have to make do on their own or wither.

Private Schools Buffing Up was the headline in the Boston newspaper. With the demographic numbers showing a surge in high school age population, attracting a larger segment of that population to the private schools makes sense. In the competition for the best of the crop, the competition often leaves losers in the public school field, another casualty of privilege.

Schools, public and private, are dependent on good teachers. Because the law mandates education to a point, institutions to provide that education compete for those teachers. Why would a teacher choose one school over another? And if students and their parents had a choice, what determines that choice? Buffing?

A buffed up school will attract potential students. This does not mean the schools neglect their internal workings; a school's reputation can slip if it does not have good programs. If the teachers and students are not happy, that will show up on the tour for the prospective applicant; and while the appearance can still be an important factor, if all schools are buffing up then the gilt becomes less significant. But the competition between public and private schools can be an unfair contest. Money does make a difference.

Athletics are an integral part of most private schools, and while the arts and extra-curricular opportunities may vary within the private school group they are usually more fully supported there than in most public schools. That commitment to the arts and extra-curricular opportunities, as well as to the athletics, encourages many people to look at something that is going to cost them a lot more money on top of the regular taxes they pay to support the public schools. A number of people have those financial resources, some stretch and sacrifice to have it happen, and some benefit from the financial commitment of the schools themselves through financial aid.

My job as Dean has little to do with this philosophical discussion, but my role as Dean has much to do with it. It would be too crass to say that I am working to buff up the internal appearance of the school, but in practice that is part of what I am doing. Appearance can belie what is happening beneath the surface, but appearance can also reflect what is happening near the core.

If we look good we feel good; if we feel good we look good. Which comes first?

For teenagers, looking good is pretty important. When we take away some of those important opportunities to look good we put more kids at risk for other problems. At a special school for students having difficulty in regular public school in a nearby city, a student knifed a respected teacher to death. The conflict was over whether the student could wear a hooded sweatshirt.

Here I am talking more about the opportunity for positive public feedback, not whether they can wear their Red Sox cap backwards in math class. Although the hat may signify looking good to some, kids in our school have more options where they can shine. Even the dedicated hat wearer will admit that the hat is not really that important. All our extracurricular activities are opportunities to "look good".

Can we afford to keep them? Can we afford not to? They do cost money, they do involve time, they do require energy. They do positively impact students and our society. How do we prove that? The utility argument is perhaps a philosophic one; what is the practical or useful worth of extracurricular activity? Can we scientifically or statistically prove that adults have more creativity, more communication, more empathy, more appreciation, more perspective on life because as teenagers they were actively engaged beyond academic and material work? I suspect social psychologists can point to studies that show that connection. As the Dean at my school I can only point to anecdotes and a personal sense that such a conclusion is indeed valid.

Although I have sometimes commented in a humorous manner that art is therapy for kids, I have seen many of our students direct their energies away from more troublesome activities to drawing, painting, dance, writing and the theater. The same can be said for students in the sports program. Many teenagers find interests and talents that they never knew they had, and thus they find success and build self-esteem. Others work out their internal struggles in a medium that thrives on expression.

Capitalism plays its part in this conflict as well; the choice of the marketplace has often become more evident in the competition for students between public and private schools. One argument could very well be that the arts are specialized and that if the minority wants to pay for it let them do so. Let them go to private school. The same argument can be used for sports; but there is money to be made in sports, even at the high school level.

The arts require hard work. There is often the sense that creative energy is the only element in art. The teachers of creativity know differently. A comment slip to my advisee from her painting teacher:

"I think you are struggling with the subject matter you selected and chose to do. Perhaps you need to rely on some pictures as a starting point and then make a departure from the pictures. So far I don't get a real feeling about the industry of fishing towns and the scenes behind that world. You are doing generic paintings of anywhere and you seem lost. There is a lot of preparation work to do before one sets out on a big venture like a Directed Study in painting. I think you need to research more and develop your pictures or go find books that will help depict the scenes you want. It requires some effort on your part."

Art is not a soft option, at least at my school.

If young people can learn more about themselves and the world they live in through the arts, then our society benefits as do the individuals. My advisee will learn not only about painting, but about the topics of her efforts, about hard work, about follow-through, about herself. What I remember about Algebra II is insignificant, but the process of learning about it had value.

I am only the Dean at a small school. Jonathan Kozol is still working hard on his crusade. The casualties continue to mount, but I would still say there is some progress in the rescue efforts.

THE GIFT

Yvette, who was a freshman girl, wandered into her proctor's room one evening in October. It was during Study Hall. The proctor was studying, but she put down her book and waited for the question. The girls were supposed to be in their own rooms from 8-10 PM so that everyone could have the opportunity to study during an enforced quiet time. Studying was not mandatory; it was, after all, something only a self could do.

"Can I ask you a question?"

"Want to ask another one?" The proctor had heard a teacher use that response earlier in the day and though it would be a good comeback for the freshman.

"Huh? Oh, yeah. Can I change roommates?"

"I thought you and Ellie were getting along fine."

"Well, we were, but . . . ."

Thirty minutes later, the freshman finally left. She had unburdened herself on the senior, venting her frustrations not only at her roommate, but also at the school, her parents, her teachers. But she felt better. Someone who had more experience than her had simply listened sympathetically. Her peers had offered opinions, advice, sympathy, even solutions—all different. What she had received in the half hour was an opportunity to work out her own solutions.

Her last words had been, "Thanks, I know you have a lot of work to do. I guess I can go finish mine now."

She didn't change roommates, and in fact she and Ellie roomed together as sophomores.

In April of her sophomore year, Yvette asked her friend Jenny, a proctor as a junior, if she thought she might have a chance to be a proctor as a junior the next year. Jenny said "Why not? You just apply and see what happens. The dorm head likes you, you're a good student, you're not on Probation, you only have a couple of room confinements. You're as good as anyone else who might apply."

Yvette thought that made sense. She had had one experience with alcohol, but she had not gotten caught, and she had been room confined a couple of times for being out of her room at 10:30 PM and for being in someone else's room during study hall. Almost everyone had that on her "record." Her peers liked her. People asked her for advice. She listened well. Why not?

The application was due on April 15th so she wrote up her statement, had an interview with one of the Deans and a couple of dorm parents, and waited until May 15 for the announcement at Assembly. Her dorm would have four proctors, and Jenny would remain as one of them, but there were some strong juniors who wanted to be proctors. Nevertheless, sometimes seniors did not want to live with freshman so she thought she might have a chance in that dorm because it was where the freshmen girls all lived. She thought she might like one of the small dorms, but she knew she would not get either a single or a proctorship in one of them for the next year.

The night before the assembly announcement her dorm head came into her room when Ellie was out and told her that although all the proctors for next year would be seniors—it was a particularly strong group of girls—that she would be the first alternate if a spot opened up.

Yvette was disappointed, but she understood, and she appreciated the news before it would be a public announcement. She could deal with her disappointment privately.

In November of her junior year one of the proctors got caught drinking. That girl lost her proctorship, and Yvette was elevated to proctor. She still had a roommate. The senior, now a former proctor, kept her single room.

In May when the end of the school year was approaching all the students began to think not only of summer vacation but also of the various awards that would be bestowed at the end of the year. Yvette told her friend Jenny that she thought Jenny would win the White Blazer award, the recognition of the outstanding senior girl. Jenny knew she would be a candidate, but she only smiled and shrugged her shoulders. It was a decision others would make. Nevertheless, Yvette was excited for her.

In September, Yvette, finally a senior, started her second year as a proctor in the same dorm. She was now a four-year senior, and she had lived in the same dorm all four years. She had a single room, friends in all the other dorms, but there were only two other seniors in her dorm—both proctors. They were both her friends, and in some ways she liked that she had more friends in other dorms because it minimized her distractions. She had plenty of work to do: two Advanced Placement classes, varsity soccer, college application essays to write, the yearbook to work on, and the responsibilities of her proctorship.

In October a freshman girl walked into her room during study hall and asked if she could talk about what a jerk her roommate was. After thirty minutes Yvette was able to persuade the freshman she should go back to her room and finish her studying for the evening and come back and talk later if she wanted to. Yvette remembered that she had not actually had the follow-up conversation she should have had three years earlier when she was the freshman talking.

In January one of her friends was sitting with her in the snack bar during their free period. She had just finished her philosophy class and was feeling a little blue.

"Do you realize how insignificant we are? He put this little pill bottle of sand on the desk and asked us to consider the grains of sand. Then he said, think of all the grains of sand in all the beaches and sandboxes on the earth. Now understand there are more stars in the universe than there are grains of sand on earth!"

The proctor smiled. She had heard the same story from a senior friend the year before. She asked, "What happened next?"

"Class ended. Why are you smiling? It's sooo depressing!"

"I heard the same story last year. I think he then took a grain of sand and asked the class to examine that single grain. You know, you never find just a grain of sand. It's always with other grains,

and each one is not only unique, it has been shaped by the ones
next to it and it shapes each one touching it."

"So you like being just a grain of sand?"

"Do I have a choice?"

When May came and the discussion turned to end of year
awards, Yvette's name was prominent among students in the
discussion of the White Blazer. She would have been proud to win
it, but she remembered her application process for proctorship
during her sophomore year and Jenny's reaction to being a
candidate the previous year.

Yvette also thought back to that October evening when she
was a freshman. She hoped that senior proctor, who had graduated
three years before, would come to graduation this year, although
Yvette knew she probably wouldn't. She knew the proctor had
given her a gift that night three and a half years earlier, and she
wanted to give one back: a personal Thank You. Yet Yvette knew
she herself had given many such gifts during her years as a student.
Some had even been acknowledged.

She could wait for graduation day.

LEARNING TO DEAL WITH A.D.D.

A.D.D.—Attention Deficit Disorder—and A.D.H.D.—Attention Deficit Hyperactivity Disorder—have become familiar terms to schools and parents over the last decade. With those acronyms came drugs to deal with them, most notably Ritalin. There are now others, but Ritalin is perhaps the most widely recognized by the public. It is a stimulant that ironically does the opposite for kids with these disorders. Ritalin allows them to focus, to gain control, to behave and to study like their peers. For those who do not have the disorder, the drug acts like the more commonly known term speed. When I was becoming familiar with the disorders and the drug, I learned that it was referred to—in the yearbook at the end of one year—as Vitamin R. It became a popular black market drug in school, and we had to deal with it on several levels.

Certainly one major change we made came when we decreed that we would treat A.D.D. and A.D.H.D. as educational rather than medical issues. This redefinition enabled us to insist on disclosure on our medical forms and in our admission process. While A.D.D. or A.D.H.D. can be a major problem for an individual student, it can also be a major problem for the community as a whole. But it does not have to be. As with any other medical issue, recognizing it, acknowledging it, and dealing with it help us address what we can do about it. Denying it helps no one.

For the first several years of my Dean's responsibilities, we saw parents struggle with wanting to keep the condition a secret to prevent a stigma from being attached to the student with the disorder. The condition did not show up on medical records, and sometimes we found ourselves working with a student who simply was too disruptive for us to keep. We actually used one student as a kind of model to assess for ourselves how we should address A.D.D. and A.D.H.D. both with students and parents. Ultimately, that particular student was beyond what we could do for him, but as with many situations there was more than one issue at hand. He was better off at home, with his parents, than in a community like ours.

However, as a result of that test case, we moved for full disclosure from the parents. Over the course of several years we also learned what kinds of students with those issues would be successful with us. No one wants to create a situation where the end result will be failure. Natural optimism, patience, even blatant hope, enter into the decision-making process, both by the parents and the school.

While medication is sometimes vital for a student to survive and succeed, it is not a panacea. Medication is used in conjunction with counseling. Finding the right combination of medication and counseling is an ongoing process. Some parents or schoolteachers and administrators look immediately to medication. Some kids and parents want no part of counseling, either because of some social stigma attached or because they do not want to deal with other issues that may be going in within the family situation. Some students do not want to take medication because of side effects or because of the stigma attached.

As a school, we treat Ritalin and medications like it as drugs that must be administered through our Health Services. Students may not keep such medication in their possession. As a result, not only in our school, but in society in general, Ritalin is more difficult to obtain for illicit purposes. Parents would sometimes conspire with their children to have the students keep and hide the medication in their rooms. The student did not want to go to the Health Services: it was too far away, it would make him late for class, it identified him as "different", the Health Services was not always open when he needed the medication, etc. The parent wanted to help the child; we called it enabling. I think we have won that battle, but there will be individual skirmishes. The last time we discovered Ritalin in a student's room was as we were about to do a room search for marijuana or alcohol, and the student quickly produced the bottle of pills that he "was just about to take over to the Health Services for storage." The parents, in their embarrassment at the enabling behavior, illegal and unwise, quickly complied with having the medication be stored at Health Services. Following procedure was preferable to having their son dismissed from school (he had a history of other transgressions with illegal substances, some proved, others not, and he had to more room for wiggle without being dismissed from school).

This is not to say the issue of keeping controlled medications in possession of students rather than at Health Services has disappeared, but it has either been acknowledged and dealt with or gone further underground. The further underground it goes the fewer people are participating in keeping medications in their possession.

While we can track how well kids do, both academically and socially in terms of staying within school rules, and we can note the differences between when a student takes the medication and when he does not, we cannot compel them to take it. As a result, some students have to leave the school because their grades are too low or they run afoul of the system accumulating minor rule violations or major ones. Kids with A.D.D. and A.D.H.D. are at a higher risk to begin with when the potential for substance use is prevalent.

The opportunity, and in fact the necessity, of me as Dean to work closely with the Health Services personnel is important to having a better community. If a student is on important medication and needs to take that medication, I can be helpful in intervening if he does not keep appointments. The behavioral results of not complying with the medication are what will eventually involve me officially, and I try to make that clear to the student. Confidentiality is important, and so is the manner in which communication happens. I do not have to work with the physical brain, but it certainly helps me to know that someone else can.

Still, we have had students and parents not provide information that would have helped us, meaning the medical/psychological professionals, do a better job. Even after students have left us, in a couple of relatively recent cases that I know of, they have died or been hospitalized because they did not comply with what we had recommended as a school. At some point we have to let go, both physically and emotionally, but it is never easy or without sadness.

A NICOTINE FIX

The issues with tobacco I find similar to those of A.D.D. in that nicotine is sometimes a physical need, sometimes a psychological need. Tobacco is illegal in our school for students, discouraged for adults, and prohibited on the campus itself except in adult homes and in a few designated areas for staff. Tobacco is both a problem that we can deal with and a dilemma that we need to manage.

Smoke produces some telling images for me. I can see Jim Carey saying "Smokin'" in his movie; I can visualize some pompous fool "blowing smoke;" I can imagine people raising a "smokescreen" to cover up what is really going on. Most often, though, I think about tobacco and how its role has changed during the last decade.

Teenagers battle with cigarettes, although they don't usually see it as a battle, and we battle with them, because in our experience and wisdom we know the real health dangers. We as adults see the images, know the statistics, understand the power of advertising, appreciate stress, and recognize the addictive nature of nicotine. Some people will get hooked on nicotine for life, struggle to deal with it, succumb to it, literally dying from it—despite what some studies would have us believe. Studies raising doubts about the link between tobacco and health dangers are funded, coincidentally, by companies which profit from the tobacco industry. As Deep Throat so famously said in *All the President's Men*: follow the money.

Another battle we face, although it may be a greater problem with older students, especially ones in college, is that science will find a cure for cancer and that people will be able to smoke all they want, and live longer and healthier at the same time. Two of the other great goddesses for the American people (money arguably being the first among firsts), are youth and science. There is the adventure, risk-taking, sense-of-immortality, do-it-now attitude that is invigorating paired with the if-there-is-a-problem-science-will-fix-it belief. What do we know as the old generation? We of little faith!

As a school, we became a tobacco-free campus shortly before I became Dean of Students. That meant that students are not allowed to smoke, possess or chew tobacco. Enforcing this, creating disincentives, is an ongoing challenge, but we have arrived at a point we are comfortable with. I hold out no ideal hope to end the problem, but tobacco violations have become a minor annoyance rather than a major problem.

Although some independent schools extend their jurisdiction over some behaviors while students are away from the school, such as on vacation or even at home, we decided on a more limited scope. We are in a small city, and therefore students can leave the campus and go to the video store, 7-11, Brooks Drugs, the coffee shop, or a day student's home and be within sight of the school. So our rule is that students cannot smoke within the boundaries of the city. Day students who live in the city are not officially under the school's jurisdiction if they want to smoke in their own homes. Students can go to the neighboring city and hang out on the street corners, smoking all they want while contributing to air pollution, pollution of their lungs, and the artistic ambience of the neighborhood. It's not a pretty sight, but it's not illegal.

We explain the seeming contradiction by recognizing the practicalities. If the student could not smoke only on campus, then we would struggle with the sidewalks, the parking lots, or any other public places that run through our campus. The local population and businesses would not be happy, either. If we extended the ban beyond the city then we make our adult population uncomfortable because they would be intimidated by going out of town on their own time, to live their own lives, and to have to deal with students breaking a school rule.

In reality, we in a boarding school are "on duty" when school is in session. I might only have a conversation with a student if I met him or her smoking out of the school's jurisdiction. If the student, however, were smoking marijuana or drinking alcohol my response would have to be different. If a student were foolish enough to do that in a public place, risking legal consequences beyond school consequences, I have little sympathy at any rate and would not feel guilty at all about intervening.

So we have multi-tiered standards. Tobacco usage is a "minor" offense; alcohol, illegal drugs, hazing, harassment, and stealing are "major rules;" misdemeanors versus felonies in the legal world.

In the earliest years of our new rule against tobacco we struggled with the sanctions. Students had little to risk by getting caught, and they went just out of sight to have a smoke. If they got caught, we recorded it and kept track, but we were not sure how to codify it. We were having similar problems with absences from commitments.

We established a committee in the summer of 1995 to come up with some solutions, and we created a system whereby there would specific penalties for the accumulation of the "minor" rule violations. We considered terms like "demerits," but that sounded too military, and in some ways it implied its opposite: merits. We did not want to have demerits erased by good works. "Points" seemed too tied with athletic achievement. The committee decided to leave it in my hands. I eventually decided on the term Units; now we have the Unit system.

We also wanted to tie accumulated minor rule violations to major rule violations. One year we had eight per semester, with a fresh start for the second semester. Experience taught us that the number of students who accumulated seven and stopped suggested that we might be better served by not starting over in January. We came to the compromise of nine Units equaling a Major Rule violation.

Finally, we wanted to put all the minor rule violations together, which included tobacco, absences, dress code, and car violations such as day student parking and driving during the day. Smoking a cigarette was the same as skipping an assembly, wearing a hat in the dining commons was the same as missing an English class. That, too, generated discussion, but after another couple of years of refinement we feel comfortable with where we are, equating the above violations as minor rule offenses rather than differentiating among them.

The rules generated good discussion in the school newspaper as well as in other places. The student newspaper is a useful historical record, sometimes even for facts. Often it is just good copy, and like any other printed word can be taken out of context. For instance, in my first year on the job there was a long editorial under a heading about "revolution." There were several subtopics, but the one paragraph about me was pretty benign. "But we move onward. [this followed a paragraph about a teacher prone to "ridiculing" the student body] The corruption does not exist simply on this level. Our Dean of Students, earns his hard earned salary sitting at the tracks, on the prowl for those damned smokers." This was more personal than it needed to be, but it dealt with a good topic. Many years after that editorial, the "tracks" are a non-issue, tobacco violations are significantly down, and the consensus that tobacco use has little merit in any area is stronger.

The "tracks" were the old railway tracks that ran about 100 feet from the dining commons, my office, the gym and the hockey rink. I do not think anyone has caught a student smoking at the "tracks" for several years. The students have gone further from campus, and they are smoking less. We feel that is an improvement.

We have lost several students over the years because they could not break their smoking habit, but our philosophy is clear, our rules are clear, our consequences are clear; this was not the right school for some of those students. Usually, smoking was connected with other issues as well: poor academic performance and drug use were the two major ones. When students would walk a quarter of a mile during the school day during a free period to have a cigarette, they were spending a great deal of time on unproductive activity. That quarter mile versus 100 feet was not insignificant. It also meant that deans would also take that quarter mile trip—sometimes we did it in our cars to save time and energy and to cover our approach (the unmarked police car—sort of).

Sometimes it was a "game," like hide and seek with relatively minor consequences. When we had the half hour in the evening after study hall when students could go out, they often went out for a smoke. One of the favorite spots was behind the old railroad station, which the school now owns, which was across the tracks from the video store and on the route to 7-11. It was about 100 feet from my office. Sometimes I would make it a point to be visible at 9:30 PM to discourage kids from having an easy smoke. One night, on a cold winter evening, I decided to get on my jeans and hooded sweatshirt and mingle with the crowd. There were probably 20 students behind the railroad station, and gradually a few began to recognize me and slink off. Finally, everyone knew who I was and cigarettes smoldered on the ground as we began to have friendly and more personal conversations. It was certainly hard evidence to me that Units or not, we had a significant problem with smoking. Eliminating that half hour in the evening was another good change that helped kids avoid an easy problem.

Making smoking or lighting any kind of flame in a school building became a major rule violation with a suspension attached. Fear of fire in dormitories, aided by the occasional story in the press about student deaths at colleges and boarding schools as a result of fires, contributed to our change in standards. Of course, we then had to deal with the case of the student who left the dorm and had a cigarette on the fire escape. We also dealt with the student who opened his window and smoked out the window. Were they in the building? The practical answer is easy and they should be "convicted," but we still needed to deal with budding defense attorneys. We extended the rule to include an attachment to a building. The student after hours would be guilty either of being out of the building after check-in or of smoking in the building. We closed the loopholes.

I have had former students return to visit during their college freshman year and note the difference on the college campus with regard to smoking. Some have commented on the ubiquitous nature of smoking in college and how they miss the tobacco-free campus both for the lack of smoke and for the absence of littered butts. Naturally, those that smoked here are relieved that they are not harassed and penalized for their right to smoke, but by the time they are 18 and in college they have most likely made their decision about tobacco use. Those that are physically addicted are on a difficult track anyway, but those that are not are more conscious of their behavior, both as it affects them and the community they are in.

Nicotine is addictive, and the earlier people connect with it the more likely they will stay with it and the more difficult it will be to disconnect from it. We work with teenagers. They are still in important formative years. We as adults and as an institution need to work with them in both the preventive phase and the reaction phase. Both are part of education.

ALCOHOL AND KIDS

According to statistics issued by studies from the US Dept. Health survey of college drug and alcohol use, from 1998 to 2000 the number of cases reported by colleges to the department rose by nearly 80% for drug use and 25% for alcohol use. Nearly half of the college students have had an experience with binge drinking.

These dramatic figures could mean several things: better reporting of incidents, fewer efforts by social institutions when these students were in middle and high school, greater cultural acceptance of drug and alcohol use, and an increase in the number of students seeking help and treatment for problems. One trend that is true in the early 21st century is that colleges as a whole are paying more attention to the problems with alcohol. There are more restrictions on parties, more sanctions applied to underage drinking, more education about the effects of alcohol, more accountability for behavior, whether alcohol related or not, more commitment to having social opportunities that are alcohol free. Colleges seem to be taking back a measure of accountability for what happens in their institutions.

Nearly thirty years ago Massachusetts experimented with reducing the age for the purchase and consumption of alcohol to eighteen. The turmoil of the 1960's led to a Constitutional Amendment, #26 in 1971, giving eighteen year olds the right to vote. This seemed to mesh with eighteen year olds being drafted and given the opportunity to die in battle while serving their country. If a person was mature enough to participate in those elements of our democratic society, then surely they were mature enough to be responsible with alcohol.

Those that drafted the Constitution of the United States nearly 200 years earlier had theories about responsibility and maturity that they enshrined in the document. While they left voting requirements to the individual states, they wrote in age restrictions for service in the legislative and executive branches of the government. A person could not be less than 25 to serve in the House of Representatives, not less than 30 to be a Senator, and not less than 35 to be a President. They valued experience and wisdom that would come with age.

The states themselves were even more restrictive. There were gender qualifications (maleness), property qualifications, ethnic qualifications, literacy requirements. Most were changed over the next two centuries, but the 18th century leaders had a more narrow view of the concept of democracy than their counterparts of the end of the 20th century.

Many lawmakers felt that the changes went one step too far with the lowering of the age of consent for alcohol, and the laws were repealed. The Federal Government exerted its influence by demanding repeal of eighteen-year old drinking laws by 1984 or risk loss of federal funds for programs. About a decade after Massachusetts legalized alcohol for eighteen-year olds the state repealed the law and went back to 21 as the minimum age. The theory of maturity at age eighteen conflicted with the results of its practice. Such practices proved to be effective political pressure.

By the 21st century there is more physical evidence in studies of the brain itself that confirm that the impact of drugs and alcohol inhibit the physical maturation of that organ. The parts of the brain that coordinate and control the functions of reason and judgment are not yet fully developed. Raising the age for legal consumption of alcohol to 21 is consonant with these findings.

The largest chunk of my duties dealing with major discipline have been involved with alcohol related activities. Access is not especially difficult despite the laws. Social expectations among teenagers put a great deal of peer pressure on them to participate in drinking. The escapism that results from a mood altering substance is attractive to teenagers that are struggling with emotional issues. The challenge to the authority of the adult rules prohibiting alcohol makes it an intriguing dare. Part of my response as Dean is to sort through all of these issues while at the same time upholding the school rules and holding the institution accountable for the behavior of its students.

Many of the chapters that I have written have involved alcohol as part of the theme. It pervades our culture, it is related to many of our problems, and it is not going to disappear.

As an institution, I think we have been ahead of the curve in the last decade as we learned to deal with issues around alcohol. Colleges are beginning to take more responsibility for what happens on their campuses and with their students. They will find resistance to that effort in some areas, but overall they are moving in the right direction. That direction will result in fewer behavioral issues, more attention to emotional problems, a healthier community for everyone and graduates who will have more responsibility as adults.

Because we are dealing with adolescents and not adults in our school, the issues are different. For quite some time now we have had a prescribed response to alcohol possession and use. We have also had a disciplinary response for students caught in the presence of alcohol. While initial reaction to the latter is sometimes called intrusive, our philosophy is simple and straightforward: the responsibility for being in the presence of alcohol rests with the individuals involved. They have a choice not to be there or not to remain there. When there are situations where a legitimate exception is possible we have acted less automatically. Students have been exonerated from penalty if the merits of the individual case warranted it.

One action colleges are beginning to take is that of informing parents of student behavior. No longer is the 18 or 20 year old going to be given the independence that they had exercised previously. This is not a step backward; it is a step forward in promoting accountability.

I have had a cartoon on my office door for several years. The strip is called Foxtrot, and the scene is the teenage character at the Principal's Office for some relatively minor offense. The teenager realizes the Principal is going to call the parents, and the boy pleads in vain for a reprieve. The Principal says to himself as he watches the boy cringe at the thought of the parents learning of the offense: this is why I love this job!

I do not sadistically go to the phone to make those calls; I have often deliberately not made those calls, depending on how well I know the student, the parents, or the situation. But when I hear students sometimes angrily complain about their parents knowing about their "private" lives through intervention by a teacher or a Dean, I am more convinced we do the right thing by communicating with the parents. Crassly or realistically, the parents are paying the bill and have a legal responsibility. If "private" becomes public through behavior then it is no longer personal and private. With teenagers, parents have a legal responsibility. Our school policy results in the suspension of a student who possesses or consumes alcohol. Ideally, we want them to go home, specifically to be with their parents and to have a family response to the behavior of the student. Sometimes that is not possible because of distance; then we find an alternative place for a student to go because we think the suspension serves a dual purpose: a message to the student and a message to the community that as a school we will act when the rules are broken.

A second requirement is that the student has to have a drug and alcohol evaluation with a report sent to our Health Services; the Dean only needs to know the report has been sent. The evaluation helps the family, as well as our Health Services, determine what the level of the problem is and what the next steps should be to prevent a repeat incident. Sometimes the incident was a first experience with alcohol; sometimes it was the result of an unlucky (from the student's perspective!) set of circumstances, and occasionally it was the culmination of a long period of abuse. The recommendation from the evaluation, which must be followed, is tailored to meet the needs of the individual student.

A third automatic result is Probation, a period lasting through the remaining quarter and the following one. If the student were to commit another similar violation during the Probation period the student would have to meet with the Discipline Committee for any hope of remaining at school. That hope is between slim and none, and I always counsel the parents to withdraw the student from school rather than face a more humiliating dismissal. Usually, but not always, my sage advice is heeded. If the second violation is in the same year but past the Probation period; i.e., in the 4th quarter after a 1st or 2nd quarter offense, the Discipline Committee is likely to recommend Separation, meaning a suspension through the remainder of the year with a possibility of return the following September if conditions are met.

If another incident occurs in a subsequent year, the student is back to the first offense situation. However, a third offense in a career means a mandatory meeting with the Discipline Committee.

All is communicated in writing to the parents, after telephone or now email correspondence. Disciplinary sanctions are also outlined in the Student Handbook, which is sent home during the summer and then additionally given personally to boarding students when they arrive. We ask the parents to keep the book at home so they can consult it.

Systemic responses are nothing new for secondary schools, but they are for many colleges and universities. Such responses are also appearing in the context of the larger environmental issues, again an area where secondary schools have been more active. In addition to education about the dangers of alcohol use, and its more nefarious cousin abuse, educational institutions are more active in promoting and providing activities that are alcohol free. Related to this are tobacco-free dorms, a recognition both that people want to live in smoke free environments but also want to avoid being around the temptation of peers that do participate. If smoking or drinking appears to be the norm, then most people, teenagers even more than adults, want to feel part of the norm.

In my school we have tinkered with the systems and the environment every year, but certainly in the last decade we have made good progress in establishing an improved community, not perfect by any means, but improved. Much of that improvement has been as a result of our increasing awareness of the issues, some to our more active intervention and response, and some to our commitment to educate our students. And one area where I know we have been more active is with our day student population.

As we became more pro-active on campus, we have seen greater involvement by our commuters. They always have had greater access to sources of alcohol, except perhaps for those periods immediately after a vacation when boarding students would return to campus with alcohol from home. Commuters now have become even more mobile and more involved with our residential students. With a school of more boarders than day students, but also with a large number of commuters, the connections made by each group with the other have grown stronger over the past ten years. The positive element in this represents the breakdown of stereotypical images of each other and the commonality of experience. When as a school we reintroduced Saturday classes nearly twenty years ago, the outcry by the commuting parents was strong. There was an underlying sense that Saturday classes were implemented to prevent boarding students from getting into trouble on Friday nights; after all, as a group they were the ones sent away by their parents because they could not do well at home. Opinions like that take some time to dispel. What we have found is that day student parents have the same issues with their teenagers, but some are in denial, some are in complicity, and some are just simply naïve. Not all of them have had an awakening, but I have seen more evidence that day student parents have become more aware of issues with alcohol.

Our boarding students can sign out for weekends, with a couple of exceptions, like the ones just before and after long breaks. Some schools have more restrictive weekend policies, some less. We require written parental permission on a form, and then we require the host for the weekend, including a parent if the student signs out to go home, to call the Dean's Office and leave a specific invitation to anyone going to the house. Students intending to take a weekend must sign out a form as well, and all the appropriate permissions have deadlines as to when they need to be done.

With the growing interaction between boarders and day students, the number of weekend signouts to local families has grown significantly over the last decade, a trend generally seen as positive. In most cases it is a terrific opportunity for a change of scenery, a time to relax from the pressures of a dorm life, and a chance to simply do some different kinds of activities that may not be available on campus or through the Activities Office. It has also been an opportunity to take advantage of parents who may not be as attuned to teenage activity as boarding school personnel.

Some people live in very big houses. They are large enough so that parents can live at one end of the house and kids can have a party at the other end and never the twain shall meet. Or the downstairs play area may be the sanctuary for the teenagers; parents do not want to intrude.

Dear Mrs . . . .

Last Saturday night you hosted several students at your home for the weekend, including a freshman and sophomore girl. During the following week we learned that there had been alcohol consumed at the house after you went to bed. All the students admitted participating when they were confronted this week.

Because of the nature of the circumstances under which we learned of the incident we are not pursuing further disciplinary action, but we are notifying the parents what happened. We hope they will speak directly to their children about our concerns and theirs and that there will be no further difficulties.

However, one consequence for your son will be that he may not host any students for overnights for the remainder of the year.

I hope we will all be more aware of the potential consequences of this kind of situation.

All the students in this situation went on to graduate.

Parents may agree that their home can be the place for the signout, but then they give the kids virtual carte blanche as to where they can go and what they can do. After all, some of these kids are nearly adults. By the 21st century the law has become much stricter, and with the rise of what we sometimes call the litigious age so has the quest for both accountability and blame. Legally the seventeen year old cannot be held responsible for what happens in the home. The parents are.

Dear Mrs . . . .

After last Saturday's incident with the student staying at your home who had to be taken to the Emergency Room, I wanted have some explicit follow-up to express our concerns and to tell you what our response has been.

The girl said she drank 13 shots of vodka in about 20 minutes and your son and his friends took her to the hospital where they called the school. After she was treated and released to your care she returned to school where she has faced disciplinary action, including a suspension.

I know you have had conversation with the parents, who live about 10,000 miles away, and have explained what happened. While the drinking took place at another home, and not under your direct supervision, our discussions about responsibility from a legal as well as practical standpoint have been frank and I hope productive. One result will be that your son will not be allowed to host students for overnights for the remainder of the year.

I was also disappointed that both your son and the girl argued there should be no school consequences because they were not under the jurisdiction of the school, having signed out legitimately to your home. However, once they called our Health Services to get assistance we were automatically involved. As the surrogate parents of boarding students we have an important responsibility to their health and welfare, and when we have knowledge of a situation it is incumbent upon us to take responsibility.

While there were both allegations and denial that there was drinking going on at your home without your knowledge or approval, if there were legal consequences to underage drinking they would fall on you as the home owner. The same consequence certainly would be true of your son's friend at whose home the girl eventually passed out; the parents there would be liable.

We were all fortunate that the girl was admitted in time and that she was treated appropriately. I am glad you were able to spend time with her at the hospital and to insure her well-being. Sadly, in some ways, she does not remember much of what happened. While others were scared and will have memories of the event, she was oblivious.

I hope we have all learned lessons from this incident and that we will not have anything like it again.

The boy did not graduate, getting into further trouble later in the year, possession of alcohol included. The girl had further difficulties as well, but of a different nature, and she was sent home for a period of time but returned to graduate.

Both of these incidents occurred at the homes of single parents, parents who were not only struggling without a partner to assist them but perhaps also too quick to be popular with their sons. Parenting under any circumstances is difficult; under these situations it was even more so.

Parents are sometimes allies in the disciplinary process, sometimes not. At another school a varsity girl athlete was benched for the Saturday game for some transgression. That night she and two of her teammates imbibed and they were caught. When told of the incident, the parents responded: "What do you expect! She was benched for the game that day!" I wonder what they expect from a school.

For every story that I might hear about officially I hesitate to think of the ones that I do not hear about. In a small community, word inevitably leaks out about incidents because someone involved wants to let at least one other person know what happened. And from there information is a communicable disease. Sometimes it lays dormant for a while, sometimes it breaks out like a pox all over the campus. The story often gets back to me at one point or another, partially because someone wants me specifically to know, partially because I might hear a snippet and then do some probing, often getting far more than I bargained for.

What is frustrating is when people give me a morsel but want to say no more. They want me to know something, but they do not want me to act. They want to give me hints, but they don't want anyone to get into trouble. They want me to make sure that their name is not linked to the information, but they want me to do my job as the Dean of Discipline. Sometimes they are parents who would like not to have to do that part of parenting.

Once in a while there is some self-righteousness in the tone of the parental confidante; their children would never be involved but some of their friends are. I have had occasion to get back to the parent with information that drinking took place at his or her house, while they were in fact home and supervising. There is no point in rubbing it in. The reality chagrins and chastens them, or they will blame someone else anyway and I only end up alienating a parental ally that I know I can use. I have seen wonderful kids involved in disciplinary incidents; I have known troubled kids who never were caught.

In one example of the situation I just described I also made a deal with one of the miscreants, a boy whose mother I knew would be appalled to learn that he had imbibed. For him the situation had been relatively minor: I had found out after the fact, and I decided that the connection I could make with him would be worth the non-disclosure of all the details to his worried mother. He had two years to go, and I gambled that I would be more rewarded with his graduation than with a family crisis that I felt he did not need. Because it was a Dean situation rather than a school disciplinary situation, because it had taken place while he was legitimately signed out for the weekend, I had some leeway. If he made another mistake, he knew he would have no further sympathy. This was what I call a risk for gain rather than a risk for loss.

A letter I received from a friend who received it from another school's Head better describes the risk for loss.

Dear Upper School Parents,

One of our students, [a]12ᵗʰ grader . . . , has suffered severe head injuries and remains in a coma at [the hospital]after an auto accident early on the morning of . . . . There were no other vehicles or individuals involved in the accident.

[His] accident has hit the school community hard. On some days, there have been 40-50 . . . students, faculty, and parents at [the hospital], everyone praying for and hoping for good news that hasn't come yet. His parents . . . have been living at the hospital and, as always seems to be the case in times like this, spending their time supporting those of us who think we are supporting them. They have been magnificent with other parents and with many of your sons and daughters.

At this moment, no one knows for certain what lies ahead for. That may change by the time you get this. In any event, we will talk about the accident with students when we get back . . . . I will speak with the Upper School first thing in the morning that day, and with the Middle School at their morning assembly on Friday.

[He] had just completed 6ᵗʰ grade when [his friend] died in an all too similar accident two weeks after his graduation; in many ways the stories are identical: a party, alcohol around, car keys taken, plans to spend the night, early morning decision to go home, losing control of a car, hitting a tree. Though [the other boy] died and [he] is alive, the guilt and grief are the same, deep and very painful, and other emotions are sure to follow. The guilt comes from those of us who feel we could have done something to prevent this accident from happening.

Some adults have told me that underage drinking is "just the way it is" or that kids who drink are "just being kids" or that "they're going to be exposed to drinking in college soon, so they

*might as well learn about it now." A student at the hospital
called it "the way of the world," as though we can only throw up
our hands and accept it. I know I've written many of you before
about this, and spoken to your children about it, but I'm going
to say again anyway that that kind of thinking is asinine. It's
irresponsible at best and gutless and dangerous at worst. If there
were something in the water supply that killed dozens of . . .
teenagers every year, or if there were a sniper picking off . . . high
school students every couple of weeks, we wouldn't say that's just
how it is. We would insist that some authority put a stop to those
killings. In the matter of teenage drinking, that authority is
parents.*

*On Wednesday morning, I will tell Upper School students some
of these same things. I will also talk about the fact that, yes,
adults do have experiences that give them better judgment than
they had when they were teenagers, just as these students will
have better judgment than their children will. With that better
judgment, adults are obligated to help kids make some decisions
or to make some decisions for them. I will ask them to stack up
whatever alcohol they may have consumed in their lives so far
and all that they might conceivably consume in the next three-
to-seven years before they become legal drinkers, and then ask
them if they would trade all that to have sitting with us in
[here] instead of lying in bed at [the hospital]. Of course they'll
know they would make that trade in a second, but we only
think like that after it's too late. I will also talk about the
absurd concept of human invincibility, ask why [his] or [the
other boy's] accident can't or won't happen to any one of us, and
try to pound home the fact that our actions under the influence
of alcohol often deny our sober good judgment. Finally, I will tell
them something about being a parent, about how much parents
love their children, and about how staying safe is one way those
children can show they understand that. Please continue that
conversation with your children when they get home and through
the coming years, and pray for [him].*

The boy died.

Courage is leadership in the face of prevailing opposition. The Head had made a public stand and used his bully pulpit to tell parents that they needed to take responsibility and make the tough choices. He was not arguing for societal abstinence, and I don't know what his personal drinking habits are. But he made a clear and unequivocal statement that people under the age of 21 were breaking the law, that they did not have the maturity and judgment of a fully developed adult, and that parents needed to take responsibility for their children obeying the law.

I have heard of parents at our school performing services for students: getting the alcohol, "supervising" the party, holding the keys, keeping the kids in one place. For the last several years we have sent out a letter during the second semester stating our explicit objection as a school to any such party, trying to help inform parents of their responsibilities and the consequences that could happen to them as adults. Our institutional support for this position is helpful to parents who are afraid to say no. The letter guarantees nothing, but it helps.

BRAINS IN SCHOOL?

As with the issues of alcohol, nicotine, A.D.D. and A.D.H.D., understanding the chemical, biological and psychological nature of maturity helps in coping with them. More and more information about the working of the brain helps us understand why people do what they do. We have seen studies of learning behavior to know that the early years of life, even while the fetus is developing in the womb, has an impact on how that child will be as a teenager. Now we are seeing more conclusive evidence that the teenage brain is still developing and that dealing with that age group ought to be different from dealing with adults. We can have a better understanding of how we should respond when there is behavior we do not like.

My own intuition led to my philosophy of: don't give me your sixteen year old and say fix it; it has been broken a long time. This intuiting seems to have been confirmed by the studies that have shown scientifically how the brain continues to change. We worry about peer pressure, as indeed we should, we worry about the media's influence, we worry about parental involvement, or perhaps more properly lack of involvement. Not that we have less reason to worry, but we might now have access to more tools to help us understand and then deal with the problem.

The "think first" approach is certainly a good philosophy, and educators have been preaching that sermon for years. Whether it be use of drugs and alcohol, throwing snowballs, crossing the street or staying up all night to play video games or study for a test, the sermon seems not to sink in, or at least not enough. We know that each year there will be a significantly large number of students new to the school, so we understand why we need to make the same pronouncements annually. What frustrates us is to have the make the same pronouncements weekly! Maybe we will simply have to do that because of the nature of the teenage brain.

This does not mean that I am using the hardwiring of the brain as an excuse for behavior. I am simply acknowledging that the brain is indeed an organic, developing factor in the decision-making process of teens. I recognize this factor, and perhaps my own reasoning is part of why I can stay relatively calm when we see foolish, unnecessary mistakes continue to occur.

One particular issue that frustrates all of us at school and our neighbors is the issue of crossing the street. My six year old is far better at waiting at the crosswalk and being sure that cars are stopped before she crosses than the teenagers at the school. This phenomenon boggles the mind. Perhaps the teenagers are not cognizant of what they are doing, perhaps they have other pressing issues on their minds, perhaps they simply have that youthful arrogance that makes them think vehicles will automatically stop for them or that they cannot possibly be injured, perhaps they are naïve enough to think that just because the law exists that says vehicles must stop for pedestrians in the crosswalk that in fact vehicles will stop. Perhaps the answer literally lies in the way the brain is functioning at that time in their lives. I will await someone's careful research before I accept any conclusions. Nevertheless, we are both fearful and frustrated by the behavior. We almost wait for the first accident of the year in hopes that it will not be so serious that the victim is permanently injured or dead but also serious enough that people may pay heed.

We have not had a death yet, but we have had some serious injuries, and we have read about deaths in the neighboring college town. We have had a student go home in November, not to return for the remainder of the year because he ran in front of a car and was severely injured. He in fact had not seen the car because another car had stopped for him. The second car simply swerved around the stopped car because the driver did not see the student crossing. The student had done the right thing up to a point.

We have had several students go to the hospital with varying degrees of injuries, some just precautionary trips, some to repair seriously damaged bones or joints. Sometimes it is not the fault of the student. I do not want to "blame the victim" because sometimes accidents do happen. But taking care to cross the street requires some forethought. It includes assessing the speed of the vehicle, the distance it is from the crosswalk, the degree of darkness, the conditions of the road—wet or icy—and the attitude of the driver. That is a significant amount of information to process. The six year old does not in fact process all the information. She just knows to stop and wait. The adult usually knows to process all the factors—not always doing so, of course—but perhaps the teenager literally is not fully equipped to do that all the time.

The decision-making process is a complex one, and the sense of time plays a role as well. There is the here and now, and there is the "later," everything after now. "Later, dude" seems to be the vernacular good-bye of the teen. The indefinite nature of that conclusion to whatever had been happening reflects the common and convenient division of the world into two parts: here/there, me/other, black/white, good/bad. Not only is that an easier way to think, eliminating all that fuzzy gray between the two clear-cut extremes, it may indeed reflect that the pre-frontal cortex is still developing a clearer sense of the future—forethought. Teenagers have forethought and the ability to plan; I know that as the Dean. Weekend activities are not exclusively spontaneous. Nevertheless, I think the not yet fully developed brain plays a role in understanding consequences. Sometimes between here and there is an intersecting variable—a car—that has not been figured into the equation.

Another issue with the traffic is the community impact. I get calls every year from a passing motorist or a neighbor or the police to let me know that students are not using the crosswalks, not looking where they are going, not respecting the boundaries of private property, not using the crossing lights, or not being respectful of motorists. The problem then becomes one of public relations as well as safety. A police sergeant called me one day to tell me how he almost ran over a student because she walked in front of his private vehicle while he was stopped at the stop sign.

She was petite and did not stand as tall as the hood of his truck. He was stopped, so she crossed; but he almost did not see her. Police and school officials are generally in concert as to the issues so we are fortunate to have a good working relationship in the best interests of everyone.

I try to respond to all of those calls, noting to the caller that we preach the "Think first" sermon and that the most helpful information for us is if we can identify individuals. My own experience is that the face-to-face conversation with the individual or group of kids has much more of an impact than the lecture. Two things happen: one is that people tend to listen when someone is talking directly to them, unlike the assembly where there are 500 people "listening" when I lecture, tell anecdotes or even do something dramatic to get attention. I know at least someone will not be listening. Second, the listener, the teenager in particular, feels respected by the personal conversation, providing that the speaker allows and expects a response. I know that most of the time a stern lecture might just get a response like a blank stare or that ubiquitous 21st century reaction: "whatever!" I need to have the last word, but how I have that last word is also important. Even a "thanks for listening" will leave the teenager feeling better— and hopefully more educated. It is certainly more difficult for the motorist, whose adrenalin is probably too high and who does not know the kids, to have that productive conversation. The teenager may be quite ready to test the authority of the anonymous motorist because the motorist appears to have no clout. The police officer, the Dean or a dorm parent is more likely to have success.

The brain is a fantastically complex piece of organic equipment, lodged in a reasonably large skull that protects it. Both grow, but the brain itself continues to grow even if the skull is finished. What happens if some other substance takes up space in the brain— perhaps some form of fluid—and pushes out on the skull? It now seems that certain parts of the brain do not have the capacity to mature because of lack of space due to the fluid. And those are the parts that are still developing in teenagers, the parts that finalize the mature person's ability to reason and help understand future consequences of present actions. Teenage skulls—thick as they may appear to be!—are still awaiting expansion of the brain. Something may not be able to develop fully. In addition to natural immaturity, organic reasons may provide the explanation for such serious matters like depression and schizophrenia.

I am thinking that with the additional millions of dollars that will devolve to me from the sale of this book that I will purchase an MRI machine for our Health Services, hire a qualified researcher, and host philosophic and ethics conferences to discuss the consequences of being able to examine the physical brains of our students. We could keep growth charts as the students progressed through the school, predict where our problems might occur, demonstrate to students and their parents what is going on with their kids that seems inexplicable to the rational adult.

While this all sounds too much like a Brave New World, no one will argue that understanding teenagers more thoroughly is a bad thing. How we go about doing it may be more the question. Certainly having access to more knowledge about the brain, about the impact of our culture on teenagers, about the individuals themselves, about the family structure and about our school structures help the educator and thus their charges—the students in the school, the young people in the village.

I think some parents might be willing to reflect on what was going on in their own brains at that stage as well. Such empathy—understanding what is happening with their children from the child's perspective—is a good thing for all aspects of schooling.

We know that exercise is a good thing for the body. We also know that exercise for the brain is an equally good thing. Schools are not simply institutions where instructors add a body of knowledge to the individual's growing internal encyclopedia; they are places for students to safely test the knowledge they are acquiring. That means the teachers, and I use "teachers" in the broad sense to include coaches, administrators, dorm parents and advisers, need to be part of the structure. Just as the physical brain is encased in a structure that has limits, so too are students part of a structure of a school, and teenagers in general are part of the structure of a village.

In schools, where peer group influence is particularly strong, a tremendous amount of active learning is going on beyond the classroom. Kids are testing out ideas and behaviors all the time with their peers. This experiential learning is in general positive, but is much more likely to be positive if it is confirmed, or at least monitored, by the adults.

When students get together to talk about any debatable issue, they are exercising their brains. But they need to know that the exercise is positive and not harmful. Coaches are asked to be up to date on strategies, training, and sport psychology by attending clinics or at least sharing ideas with their peers. Classroom teachers and school administrators are asked to do the same thing. A student can be physically injured by improper training techniques, by using the weight room apparatus inappropriately, by surpassing safe limits. Poor teaching can have an adverse effect on a student's future by teaching or reinforcing harmful attitudes.

Although certainly not exclusive to teenagers, the tendency to end an argument with ad hominem statements ("you are wrong because you are stupid"), focusing on the individual rather than the question at hand, frustrates teachers and leads to personal confrontations rather than intellectual ones. Adults and students alike can conclude that immaturity causes the breakdown in the process of debate. The "agree to disagree" conclusion is difficult for the incomplete brain and the ideologue alike.

With the pre-school aged child we know that the disputatious event will quickly be forgotten. We often argue that with the teenage boys it will also be effectively forgotten, but with teenage girls we feel it lingers and festers. In the boarding school atmosphere where peers live in close proximity, the adults have to manage not only the argument itself, which may be about some important ethical issue or something seemingly petty, but the way it is discussed and concluded. Parents work with this kind of conflict within the family, but it most often is with the teenagers' siblings. In a school, and especially in a residential program, the conflict is with peers from different families and perhaps even with greater differences, like race, religion and culture. That strikes me as a great deal of pressure on a still developing brain.

I watched conflicting opinions develop over issues like the OJ Simpson trial, the Monica Lewinsky/Bill Clinton saga, the '96 election campaign, issues raised in ethics class, and sometimes in my own classes about Hitler and Nazi Germany, Philosophy or US History. I am reminded of the view we sometimes have of American travelers going to a foreign country and, not familiar with the local language, persist in trying to communicate in English but using two important modifications: raising the voice and speaking slowly. When teenagers get into difficult debates the volume usually rises, but the pace goes faster rather than slower. In hindsight I have reflected on those classroom situations where the discussion got out of hand and how I was challenged to get back on track.

We had two boys on opposite sides of any issue living in the same dorm, and one was better at needling the other. So of course the victim of the needling, tired of the harassment that persisted despite warnings to discontinue, punched his tormenter one day outside the library. The damage was not horrific, but of course the school had to respond, so we wrote letters, made up contracts and survived the rest of the year. Would the MRI have showed anything?

Two girls, falling out after boyfriend changes, continued to talk about each other endlessly, creating constantly swirling eddies down the stream of school life. They changed rooms, one changed dorms, and allies were formed on both sides. The adults wanted to scream: Get over it! Move on!

The village has many soap operas, but somewhere the physical brain is playing a part, and we know we will have similar struggles in the next school year. There is plenty of discussion in the media about the cultural and social influences on teenagers, and we almost randomly read or see information seeking to inform and instruct us on how to work with teenagers. I use random because there is too much to absorb, and we each come across some article or program we think everyone should know about. As we add more about the organ of the brain we are including yet another important topic.

More and more and more. Maybe parents send their children to
schools because they think the school personnel know all this stuff
while they don't!

While the brain is not going to be physically injured by
argument and debate, it certainly can be permanently damaged
by chemical changes induced by drugs and alcohol. The developing
brain, not completely formed in the teenage skull, is susceptible
to long-term damage by chemicals, just as it would be from a
physical blow to the skull.

All that perceived euphoria or temporary high that comes with
chemical addition to the brain is having a long-term effect that is
not immediately obvious. Perhaps because we do not see the physical
effects on the brain we think that a negative effect is not really
happening. Would it make a difference if we had the evidence
from the MRI? Would the individuals care? The sense of caring is
where the physical interacts with the mental and the emotional. If
an issue distresses someone, then dealing with the distress must be
more fundamental than the particular issue. The physical changes
that occur with a chemical alteration are brought on by the
individual's choice to use the chemical because he or she was
distressed. For that individual if the distress were not present then
the chemicals would not have been used.

But if the issue is primarily a physical issue within the brain,
which it certainly can be as with pathologies like schizophrenia,
bipolar disorder or depression, then the appropriate treatment must
start with the physical and not the emotional. Discovering which
is the fundamental problem is the challenge we have in our
relationships with the troubled teenagers.

As school personnel we are becoming more aware of this diagnostic
dilemma, but educators are not trained to evaluate it. We are asked to
pay more attention to behaviors as symptoms and hope that the more
professionally trained staff members are able to help teachers,
administrators, parents and the students come to grips with what is
happening. For most teenagers, what is happening is normal growth—
which includes challenging everything in sight—but for some of
them the behaviors are something not normal.

When something is not normal and can be corrected, usually by medication but occasionally by surgery, then the individual and the family faces a choice. That choice might not be as simple as we would like it to be. Medication for one thing may have side effects in some other area. It may also simply test a student's ability to accept a change.

There is a stigma attached to some forms of medication. We make jokes about Prozac or Ritalin or Viagra, but teenagers are often more sensitive to their peer relations than adults are. Teenagers have enough problems with testing themselves in their peer sub-society without also having to explain that they are taking medication to control something that they personally cannot. This issue of control of feelings or behavior irritates most of us at varying times in our lives, but the physical nature of the brain is not something we have dwelt on in the past. While it is not my business or prerogative to know who is on what medication, the opportunity, and in fact the necessity, of me as Dean to work closely with the Health Services personnel is important to having a better community. As the endless stream of scientific, and sometimes not scientific, data crosses our paths, we sometimes have the opportunity to reflect. As an example:

Sleepiness possible root of behavior problems

> By Lindsey Tanner, Associated Press, 3/4/2002
> CHICAGO—New research suggests children who snore face nearly double the risk of being inattentive and hyperactive, providing fresh evidence of a link between sleep problems and attention deficit disorders.
>
> While the study doesn't answer whether one condition causes the other, the researchers contend that snoring and other sleep problems may be the culprit in some cases because children often express sleepiness by being inattentive and "hyper."
>
> The theory could help explain why stimulants such as Ritalin can effectively treat children with conditions like

attention deficit/hyperactivity disorder, or A.D.H.D., who already seem overstimulated, said Dr. Ronald Chervin, a University of Michigan neurologist and sleep researcher, and the study's lead author.

"If there is indeed a cause-and-effect link, sleep problems in children could represent a major public health issue," Chervin said. "It's conceivable that by better identifying and treating children's snoring and other nighttime breathing problems, we could help address some of the most common and challenging childhood behavioral issues."

A.D.H.D. is the most common neurobehavioral disorder in childhood, affecting between 4 percent and 12 percent of school-age children, as many as 3.8 million youngsters. Data cited by Chervin suggest that between 7 percent and 12 percent of children snore frequently, with apnea-brief breathing lapses during sleep that can cause snoring—present in up to 3 percent of school-age children.

Numerous studies have found a link between sleep problems and A.D.H.D., but many sleep specialists and psychiatrists are divided over which condition might cause the other.

"There's absolutely a connection," said Dr. Stephen Sheldon, a sleep specialist at Children's Memorial Hospital in Chicago. "There is a proportion of youngsters that have sleep pathology causing their daytime symptoms that appear virtually identical to A.D.H.D."

Dr. Timothy Wilens, a child psychiatrist at Massachusetts General Hospital in Boston, is more skeptical. "I would say the verdict is still out," he said.

A.D.H.D. is thought to have a genetic cause and runs in families, Wilens said. The sleep disturbances his research has found in A.D.H.D. children, including restlessness and difficulty falling asleep, are probably the result of behavioral problems, not vice versa, he said.

Chervin's study involving 866 children ages 2 through 13 is published in the March issue of Pediatrics. It is based

on surveys of parents about their children's behavior and
sleep patterns.

Parents rated behavior on a list of criteria for A.D.H.D.,
which includes impulsiveness, inability to pay attention,
and excessive activity. Parents weren't asked whether children
had been diagnosed with A.D.H.D., which Chervin
acknowledged limits generalizing the results.

Overall, 16 percent were frequent snorers and 13
percent scored high on the A.D.H.D. scale.

Among frequent snorers, 22 percent had high
A.D.H.D. scores, compared with 12 percent among
infrequent snorers.

Since snoring is often caused by apnea, which is
frequently caused by large tonsils, removing tonsils might in
some cases improve behavior, Chervin said.

Now that we know this important information, how best can
we utilize it? If only education were as simple as just teaching.

ETHNICITY

Sometimes the scientific and the affective begin to diverge in the village, sometimes they intertwine, confusing rather than clarifying. I work with some of these issues regularly, and I do not always have the experts to rely upon.

As a student body we are diverse. As a faculty and administration we are decidedly not. That has been a recognized problem for many years, and the school has taken a variety of initiatives to address the issue and resolve the glaring disparity. Success continues to elude us.

We need to have a diverse faculty for many reasons, not the least of which is to have good role models for our non-white students. Our Asian contingent is between 10-20 %, and our African-American contingent is about the same. Other international students, some with American backgrounds, are about another 10%. In the absence of good adult role models, we have cultivated some excellent role models within the student leadership group, in the last several years in particular. Nevertheless, that is a difficult burden for those kids to share on top of taking care of themselves. Several have been recognized as the outstanding students in the entire senior class with awards at graduation ceremonies; and they were awarded the distinctions because of what they did, how they acted and led, not for their ethnic background.

So our little village, diverse and successful as it is and may be, still is wanting. And, indeed, it always will be in some arena. Racism, a term sometimes used inappropriately, has been a topic in our student paper throughout my years as Dean so the issue has not been ignored. We have had articles for and against affirmative action, articles about experiences the African-American students have had on and off campus, and articles about speakers both here and elsewhere. When OJ Simpson made his famous drive down Rodeo Boulevard, we were not in school, but when the trial results came out there was the same tension and disagreement on our campus as there was in society in general. The verdict was viewed more positively by the students of color and more negatively by white students. But because of the nature of our life, other issues quickly replaced that topic. Nevertheless, it highlighted the same feelings that exist in the larger world beyond our village.

Our students of color are in most respects just like white students. They study hard most of the time, have success and lack of it in extra-curricular activities, sometimes drink alcohol or smoke dope, have interpersonal conflicts with peers and adults, are leaders and followers, express themselves openly in some areas while bottling up other issues. They have parents who are teachers or lawyers or businessmen. They are regular kids, but they have an additional factor in their being.

I have come to dislike the term race, and I use the term racism with a narrow meaning: prejudice with power. But if the term race is a political one, a view that I currently subscribe to, then racism becomes a moot point. However, replacing it with ethnocentrism is going to be hard to sell linguistically to the general public. It's too long a word; it's not catchy, sounding more like a sociologist's term rather than something the average person would use; it's not all encompassing. So we will be living with the term racism for a while.

With the scientific information exploding, genetic marking seems to be a much more accurate description of human beings than ethnic identification. Ethnic identification is identified with geography, language, religion and skin color, sometimes lumped together under the heading of culture. My sense of race is human as opposed to non-human. Within the continent of Africa there is the greatest variation of genetic difference, and thus Africans on either end of the genetic "map" might have more in common with Europeans or Asians than they do with each other. Nevertheless, if all are 99.9% the same genetically, how different is.1%?

Yet if there are 3 billion nucleotides in the human genome, 3 million are different between individuals or perhaps groups. Do we see the .1% or the 3 million? Science and politics could clash here, and that is not my area of expertise. As the Dean, I do not need this kind of knowledge for my job, but it does increase my understanding of our society. I feel I need to acknowledge my awareness of differences, and at the same time I want to find what we all have in common. I am not blind and I do not want to be racist. Sounds like a good challenge.

In the United States we have used racism ethnocentrically, and historically the issue focused on color. The percentage of blackness determined whether a person would be restricted by racially sensitive laws—Jim Crowism. After the Jim Crow laws were declared unconstitutional, prejudice still existed of course, and that pre-judging focused on color. Black culture in the United States has often been an attempt to identify a sense of separateness from mainstream white culture. This can become confusing when within the white population the German-Americans want to be different from the Italian-Americans who want to be different from the Jewish-Americans, etc. As a result of a pretty horrific history on the continent of Africa, exponentially exacerbated if not caused by European interference, African-Americans cannot attach a particular ethnic tag to the first part of the hyphenated term. Prejudice thus came most easily based on color. White ethnic groups could bond together because of who they were not (black), and black people could bond together because of who they were not (white).

In the 21st century, the difference is often one of style as the economic class differences become more prominent. The rise of the black middle class has left behind a large group of disadvantaged African-Americans. The gap between the latter group and the rest of American society, black and white, is growing steadily, not shrinking as optimists would hope. An economically middle or upper-middle class African-American teenager, as determined by income, can feel caught between what is identified as main-stream culture and minority sub-culture.

Examples of this sense of culture, and I think I am using that term in a very broad and vague sense, are language and appearance. Success for some young people, white or non-white, might be embodied in the NBA or NFL, television or movie stardom, or music video performance. While the professional sports teams are regulated by league rules, iconoclastic behavior is sometimes worth the risk of a fine. The idea of sportsmanship runs counter to trash talking and the in-your-face kind of behavior that occasionally gets highlighted. Television has even more regulation, Jerry Springer notwithstanding, but movies and videos are probably more freely governed by the marketplace: if sex and violence sells we'll produce it. We may be appalled by what in fact sells, and even though you and I may not be buying it plenty of people are. The language and appearance may not conform to polite, or middle-class, or white society, but those expressions of individualism and identity have power within the subgroup.

In the mainstream of American adult culture, however, certain ways of speaking and dressing are going to be prerequisites for success. Thus, many of our African-American students are somewhat bicultural and "bilingual." There is a black cultural norm and a majority (read white), cultural norm. NFL commentators, black or white, speak more similarly and dress more similarly than the teenage fans do. Newscasters, lawyers, bankers, business professionals, and teachers: they all have a norm that is different from the teenage norm. So our students, who want to be successful, have to learn the majority norm while at the same time not wanting to be rejected by the minority norm. All teenagers face this dilemma; African-American teenagers have a more pronounced problem.

Our African-American students have many stories of their own to tell, certainly from a different perspective than mine. While I perhaps have begun more dialogue this year as I try to examine this issue, student discussion and leadership has also become stronger. As with other issues like homophobia, drugs and alcohol, and sexuality, the eagerness to talk about race simmers. The African-American students say they have many discussions among themselves about these topics and certainly about the perspective of being non-white, but there is too little dialogue with the mainstream of white students. As with other topics, some students feel there is already too much discussion. "Do we have to have another assembly about . . . (drugs, homophobia, race, sexuality)! I'd rather do my homework." Yet I sense there is more dialogue on campus than there used to be, whether it be in class, in the dining commons, in the student center, or in the dorms. Individual students have at times resented having to represent the "black perspective" when they feel they just want to be seen as a student regardless of color, but at the same time the African-American students have had experiences that no white student will ever have. They have resented the insensitivity of the white population about prejudicial or ignorant comments or behavior, but it is tiring to have to be a representative as well as an individual.

At my school, the students are all gearing for college, and the majority norms prevail. Yet we are constantly aware that the African-American students are different from the white students, if only by the obvious distinction of color. I am the middle-class, middle-aged white male, and as the Dean of Students I think that I feel this difference from the African-American students acutely; but I try not to show it. I can dialogue with them seemingly just as easily as I can with other students, but I am constantly aware of my difference from them. That does not qualify as racism because I am not exercising power by my skin color; it is not bigotry because I am not treating them differently in a negative form; perhaps, though, it is a form of prejudice because I am conscious of a difference between us and that consciousness might lead to a prejudgment.

I know I am not alone in this dilemma because when we have had to have discipline responses to African-American students we seem to want to be even more careful that we have the facts clear. We want to be even more assured that we are not dismissing a student from the school when he or she is African-American unless we are clear that there is no perceived racism that could come back in our faces. I am sure we have not acted in a prejudicial fashion towards any of our African-American students when it has come to school discipline; but that has not prevented the concern from being raised, by either the mainstream culture or the minority population.

Another personal example of the kind of thinking that may be tainted by color-consciousness is when I am conjuring up examples of students I would like to write about. I have an easier time remembering names of the outstanding African-American students and the problematic white students. I can easily make wonderful comments about these stars, know who they are, why they were terrific. Maybe it is just numbers. If only 15% of our student population is African-American, there are numerically fewer stars. If there are 70% that are white, the stars blend together and the unique ones tend more to be the ones I have seen in the discipline process. The same would be true of the numbers of African-Americans who have been in trouble. There should be fewer and thus easier to recall. Yet I felt I have had to think harder to find the African-American problem students and reflect on their transgressions. I have not erased the names and events, just filed them further back in the memory cabinet.

Transgressions against the rules seem to place a greater burden on the prosecution (read: Dean), to prove on evidence alone. When the transgression involves other people, such as in harassment, there is often another story. The he said/she said scenario can be tricky, and it involves one side lying and persisting in the lie. There may be different "truths" in the story, but there are also facts.

A disconcerting case involved an African-American boy and a young female teacher who was one of his dorm parents. There was tension and finally there was a threatening but anonymous note. Proving that it came from the student took some time, and the intervening period was rife with tension and fear. Both sides had their supporters, but eventually we had to send the student home where he underwent counseling. His mother did not want to believe that her son could have done such a thing. It was my painful duty to give her the evidence and have the son eventually come to grips with what he had done. He did not return to school.

It was not only painful for her, but it was also painful for the teacher, who not only experienced fear but frustration. Why should her word be questioned against the word of a student? Why should she have to remain in the same building, as a responsible *in loco parentis* adult, with the student who threatened her safety?

I sometimes long for the magic wand that will make everything right immediately, but I prefer to use King Solomon as the model. He may have had to threaten to cut the baby in half to share with the two maternal claimants before he learned the truth, but he listened first, used some good psychology, and heard some pain from both women before he acted.

The "victim of circumstances" is also another good ploy that almost everyone uses, and I think we use no bias in reaching our conclusions, regardless of the ethnicity, religion or place of national origin of the accused. Another African-American student who was on our concern list eventually lost his position at the school after we did a room search and found about 50 marijuana plants growing contentedly in his closet under a heat lamp. Protests about why we did a room search fizzled quickly. Parent or school authorities could hardly accept the possibility or the claims that the plants were someone else's or not marijuana plants at all. In the long run, his mother was indeed worried, and perhaps the boy simply needed to be home rather than away at a boarding school. As with many stories, I do not know what has happened with that student after he left. I can only hope he did what we recommended and that he found academic and personal success.

A couple of other instances also involved our local police, and that too raised some concerns. We had finally caught a particular student using marijuana, and following standard procedure he was suspended and had to have the evaluation; the routine process. Not unusually, the parents were shocked and surprised, but we all survived that trauma. About two months later he was in a car with several other students, an African-American boy and two white girls, one of whom was the driver. They drove by a police officer directing traffic through a site where one lane had been closed for work. The officer thought he smelled marijuana from the car, and he called for a patrol car, which stopped the car in a parking lot near the school. A student walking by alerted someone in the school building, and I walked over to find out what was going on. The police had found enough marijuana that they were going to charge this student with possession to distribute.

The girls were both day students, the boys both boarding students. They should not have been going off in the car during the school day in the first place, one of those minor rule violations that we deal with from time to time. The possession of the drugs for the boy who was on Probation meant that he would be dismissed, but again the parents were concerned that all this was a mistake and the search illegally performed. Nevertheless, they decided to withdraw the student before we formally dismissed him. He still had court to contend with.

His lawyer successfully won the case, arguing that the evidence was unlawfully obtained because there was not probable cause to search the vehicle. Implicit was the concern that because there were two African-American boys in a car with two white girls, the car was singled out to be stopped. Not long after this, the national concern regarding racial profiling resulted in some significant changes in the way police across the country acted.

This particular student was clearly headed for trouble, and he had not heeded the warnings we administered earlier. Even later, when his court case was still pending, he returned to a neighboring city late one weekend night and showed up at the home of a day student where there was a party. He eventually was asked to leave the premises. I wondered why and how he had had left his parent's jurisdiction (his parents were divorced and he was going from one to the other), to come from several states away for this event, to which he had not been invited.

As in the case with many students who find trouble, this particular one had started fairly well. He was talented, we had targeted him for leadership even when he first arrived, and he was personable. Yet something went amiss in his term here, and he chose a different path. As always, we were saddened by his loss (of opportunity as much as anything), and we questioned where we had not done enough. That he was an African-American male added to our self-examination. What were the factors in his life that at seventeen he made decisions that closed doors for him? Maybe when he is thirty he will be able to reflect better on that. I hope he has that opportunity.

Another incident involving the local police came again with the issue of marijuana. We learned of a party that involved a group of boys, and when we investigated there was contradictory evidence. We decided to hold a discipline committee hearing because we were concerned about lying as well as learning all the facts. There were five boys involved, one of which was African-American and one Hispanic. Those two plus a third boy were Separated until the end of the year for their role in the incident, which included lying. None of them returned to the school the next year.

During the investigation we learned that the police had apprehended the African-American student several weeks earlier for possession of a joint. They had warned him and sent him on his way, extracting what information they could in lieu of prosecuting or even turning him over to the school. For the police, possession of a small amount of marijuana is not as important a concern as getting to the dealers and suppliers. They were willing to bargain with the student, and he complied. We do much the same at school if we do not have enough evidence to process. We do not make a deal over possession of marijuana because it is a clear violation of our school rules, and we are not the police looking for the sources. We are a school dealing with individual students. Most of the time the police are more than happy to turn over a student like this to us because we deal with the students both more strictly and more therapeutically than the local police or courts do. However, in this case the police had decided that they could utilize the circumstances for their own purposes, and we were not informed. When we did our investigation of the later incident, we contacted the local police to test the student's story about buying from a local dealer. Then we learned about the first instance.

When this past history came to light within the disciplinary committee process, the Committee members had little sympathy with the students, who had confessed to a pattern of behavior rather than to this one specific instance. They had both not told the whole truth, and they lied in the process to cover their involvement. They were told they could not stay at the school.

Concern was raised that students of color were treated more harshly, that the Committee did not take into account cultural backgrounds and needs, and that the police targeted them because they were students of color. While there was sentiment that the school could have suspended them and then worked with them further, they did indeed break a major school rule and then lied about it, regardless of whether their previous behavior came out. The two major offenses made them eligible for Separation. Yet if they had not been Separated, the next case with similar circumstances would need to result in the same outcome for the sake of consistency. The community at large had to have confidence in the system of discipline rather than allow this particular case to be determined separately. Because minority students were involved, ethnicity simply made this case more problematic.

I reflect on these last stories and cannot help but note that they are all about teenage boys. This was not a conscious effort on my part, but I think it highlights the ongoing challenges we have with teenage males and then compound that with the African-American background. I have no doubts about the legacy of slavery and then its follow-up period of segregation and the ongoing issues of racism topped with basic prejudice. We struggle in my school no differently than everyone else.

African-American girls have also been in trouble, but there has been markedly less difficulty with substance abuse. Theft, fraud, and shoplifting have been the primary Probationary offenses committed by African-American girls, but they are not markedly different from what their white counterparts have been involved with.

Another area of ethnic change that I have observed over the last decade has been with our Korean student population. Many American boarding schools that have Korean students experienced a cultural phenomenon that we had difficulty with. That difficulty was a distinct hierarchy, with a senior Korean male exercising significant authority and power over the rest of the group. The problem with this phenomenon was hazing. It was often well hidden by the group, difficult to prove, and challenging to break. In the last several years we have seen less of it, no doubt in part to our commitment to stopping it. This required a two-pronged attack: first, to be clear that we would not tolerate hazing and that there would be official school consequences to hazing: our cultural context would override theirs; second, to educate the students about their roles and our rules. We tried to establish appropriate leadership skills and behavior. We wanted Korean (and any ethnic), leaders to be leaders not only within their own subgroup but in the school as a whole.

Other institutional efforts include a commitment to spread the students around the boarding community and not concentrate a minority contingency in a particular dormitory. We have been doing the same for any identifiable group: athletes, age, interests, etc. We believe in diversity and the acceptance of different styles, while being intolerant of anti-social behavior. Were we being culturally insensitive to the Korean male experience by breaking down the behaviors associated with their hierarchical structure that they brought with them? Yes, but they were residents in our American culture not Korean. We were not trying to change Korea, although certainly we could argue that we were indirectly. By making clear what our rules are before students matriculate here we are offering students the choice of whether to attend or not, accepting our rules if they come.

A second commitment was to increase our efforts to have a faculty International Adviser, whose job has expanded over the last several years. This meant not only someone who would be trained to teach ESL (English as a Second Language), but also someone who would be sensitive to cultural differences and advocate for this group of students. It has certainly been easier to fill that position than it has been to attract African-American teachers to our community.

The International Student coordinator's job has a wide range of responsibilities, as does any teacher in a residential school. Prejudice and ignorance are not exclusive to Americans. Reading between the lines of why an international student's father did not want his daughter to room with an African-American student challenged our skills as educators as well as humans struggling with personal anger management. It certainly sounds easy to say: "keep your daughter home!;" but we do not want to punish the child for the sins of the father. Hopefully, the prejudice and ignorance will not be repeated in the next generation; but they may. The same student had difficulties with sexuality, alcohol, and honesty. But she made it, shakily. I am curious as to what the next chapters will be for her.

Sexuality is also a difficult subject with students and their parents who come from quite different cultural backgrounds than what we are accustomed to seeing in mainstream American life. That is not to say that we approve of all the sexuality that pervades our American culture, but it is an even greater concern for people from other cultures.

When we had a situation of sexual assault that occurred off of school grounds and when students were not under the jurisdiction of the school, we had a complicated case to navigate. The victim was reluctant at first to come forward because there was other illegal activity involved: alcohol and false sign-outs. Nevertheless, she had to confront her own psychological difficulties and ultimately became more open about the situation. The male student who assaulted her came from a significantly different cultural background. How would he be treated at home? Was that our problem? If the girl did not want to prosecute through the legal system, and that on its own may have been problematic, what should our actions and responsibility be? How did the girl want to follow up with this, not only in reference to herself but with her parents and peers as well? I was told by her explicitly not to tell her dorm parent; she felt uncomfortable with that person, who happened to be male. She was very concerned about who knew and who did not.

Sounds like a good case for cover-up. Let's bury this mess!

We could not do nothing. Both students had a future to

consider, both needed help beyond the disciplinary response of simply a Dean, both had parents who needed to get through this. Neither student needed to be thrown on the dung-heap of our history.

Through patience, hard work, listening and talking, good counseling and cooperation from the students involved we struggled through it. I would love to hear their perspective ten years later. While I am never sure we did the best thing, we certainly could have done worse. I am convinced that one way we could have done worse would have been to be more public with the details of the case. Both students, for different reasons, wanted to have a high level of confidentiality. To a large degree, we granted it. That did not mean we covered up the problems. The girl participated in counseling and the boy was suspended and was readmitted under strict conditions, which included counseling.

There are always people who want to know but should not. That situation is never comfortable; keeping those not directly involved "out of the loop" is no mean feat. They, like the students, also have both opinions and feelings. This case included the mix of ethnic and cultural concerns, alcohol, sex, false sign-out, faculty, parents, and the student community. Any of them alone could be complicated. The cultural component was important for us in dealing with the boy's situation, and we weighed that in our actions.

While we as adults know that students need role models and substitute parental influences when they are at a boarding school, we find it difficult to communicate to the students that the adults need the same kind of empathic support from peers and the community. Students may be here for four years, but they move on. Ideally, we would like teachers to stay for a long period of time, to be successful, committed, satisfied, and happy in what they are doing being in the midst of a community. Adults need mentors and support as well as the students. If they cannot get that support or give it they leave this life style.

Having an ethnically diverse faculty as well as a student body is an important goal for our school. We understand, somewhat, the phenomenon of why all the black kids sit together (*Why Are*

All the Black Kids Sitting Together in the Cafeteria? And Other Conversations About Race, by Beverly Tatum), and why the international students sit together. Who would the adults sit with if they were the sole minority or even part of a group of two or three people? Would they feel comfortable in the community if they were a visible minority, regardless of their interests in an academic discipline, athletics, or the arts? Having minority teachers is a major challenge that communities as well as schools struggle with. It is not just the students that need support.

THE HOMOPHOBIA
HOTPLATE

How difficult is it to move from the challenge of ethnicity to that of sexual preference? Again, we surf the muddy waters where science and . . . what? Belief? Emotion? Fear? . . . commingle.

Homophobia continues to be a frighteningly insidious force in our community, and in most communities. And homophobia remains a legitimate prejudice in the eyes of many.

While racism and sexism have been confronted and, if not defeated, at least put on the defensive, homophobia retains a status of acceptability in several areas: religious, social, scientific, and psychological. People, and in the school community where the largest peer group is teenagers, can make homophobic references or jokes or pronouncements with less fear of sanction than they could about people of color, about women (or perhaps men), or about ethnic groups.

In my role as Dean, I am less inclined to pontificate, to preach about the intolerant or undemocratic or cruel nature of prejudice, as much as I am to have concern about the individuals involved. I know of the statistics about teenage suicide and depression that stem from concern about one's sexuality or status in the community. I see teenagers almost every day, and certainly when school is in session I see them all day long. They do not spend their days pondering sexuality because they have too many issues right in front of them: the math test, the basketball game, the emails, the novel to read, the friendships. Yet underlying all those activities is sometimes a nagging force that erodes their sense of their own stability. Individuals or the sense of the community as a whole can push them to have behaviors that deserve our attention.

Very few teenagers are "out," openly homosexual. That is too terrifying. They may not in fact know for sure where their sexual orientation lies, but society has powerful images pushing them in one direction. Confusion and angst, common in most parts of teenage lives anyway, are exacerbated when sexual identity is part of the mix.

From time to time there are overt acts of homophobia: writings on the bathroom walls, notes pinned to doors, messages passed through electronic media or the telephone. Occasionally, there are more blatant acts: mutilation, beatings, and verbal assaults. When identified, the blatant acts are more easily addressed. They are illegal, they are against school rules, and they are against the philosophy of the particular village. But when they take on the patina of legitimacy—a discussion in class, an article in the school newspaper—they raise other issues: censorship, power, the role of education, the philosophy of academic freedom. As in many issues, the conflict is often over the welfare of the individual versus the welfare of the community. Are there times when the village should act in the best interests of the common good and sacrifice an individual? Philosophers have struggled with these issues for centuries, and we in each of our villages and schools will continue to struggle with them.

When we had a difficult issue with homophobia in 2001 as it was written about in our school newspaper, the emotions in our school community burst into full flower. What had always existed, mostly beneath the surface but occasionally open, was now directly in our collective faces. One article, written by three senior boys, equated homosexuality with pedophilia and incest.

> . . . . *There is a reason why homosexuality grosses people out and makes them uneasy. There are reasons why some states forbid gay rights. It is not because people are jerks or not understanding, but because some people understand that a gay lifestyle goes against our human being. We do not want to spread the message that homosexuality is normal or natural. We do not want to spread the message that homosexuals are good role models for how*

*children should grow up. Homosexuality can be compared to
pedophilia or incest. We do not permit these types of sexual
relationships, so why is homosexuality any different? . . .
Homosexuality, incest and pedophilia are all perversions. They
are problems that exist in the human mind. They are innate
perversions that some people are more inclined to do. We believe
they must exercise abstinence from their sexual inclination in
order to live a healthy, moral life . . . .*

*To allow gay sex and spread the message that homosexuality
is normal is, we believe, a mistake and hurtful to all of mankind.
We are not gay haters. We are not mean, uncaring people.
We are just people who will never sacrifice the right thing to say
in order to save face.*

That issue was not going to go away quietly or soon.

At our school we have several openly gay teachers, several with
partners on campus who participate in community life on multiple
levels, and at least three with children as well as partners. I can
only imagine the depth of their dismay and anger. Did the school,
through the use of the school newspaper, legitimize not just
homophobia but outright ignorance through the publication of
the letter? Despite the fact that there was a simultaneous editorial
statement, individual faculty expression of rejection of the views
voiced, and student rebuttal from our diversity group and our
Gay/Straight Alliance, all denouncing the viewpoint of the letter,
should the letter have been published?

That debate will continue. And most feel it should. Some would
like the discussion to be suppressed completely because the topic
is uncomfortable and divisive. But the issue is always there. Those
that are openly gay have courageously chosen to follow their path.
It will be a long time before that path is acceptable to everyone,
and they know they have to find the strength to stay on that path.
Our gay faculty members support each other, they have support
from non-gay members of the community, they are judged on
what they do and who they are as human beings, not on their
sexuality. But they are still gay in a world where heterosexuality is

the norm by both practice and belief. If it were not the norm, the teenage suicide rate would be significantly lower.

I enjoy Norman Rockwell's art. I am not qualified to be an art critic, but I can learn to accept legitimate critical appraisal of works of art. That does not mean I will like the particular painting, poem, musical arrangement or drawing, and what I want on my walls are things that I will enjoy because they please me, not because they please the critics.

Norman Rockwell does not have any work that I know of that addresses the issue of homosexuality. He died before homophobia became confronted and openly identified as hate-based. Homosexuality was for the most part a topic that was not addressed openly, and certainly not in mainstream conversation.

But Rockwell did take on some tough topics. I could not help but think of the painting done in 1964 with the little African-American girl going to school, surrounded by federal marshals, walking by graffiti scarred walls, passing through a hate-filled environment to get to a school. I can hardly imagine what she must have felt then. I wonder what she feels now. Was her walk to school that day worth the pain she must have endured? Would we as a society have been better off had she not taken that walk that became a journey?

On Martin Luther King Day, January 15, my kindergarten daughter learned a great deal about the honored man and some other events and people in the civil rights movement. One was a little girl named Ruby Bridges. She was the girl in the picture. She was also the subject of a book in my daughter's class. Ruby Bridges has told her story, and she has become a successful businesswoman, mother and leader in the community. Some journeys do not have a clear and defined destination. Ruby's didn't, but she would have had. quite a different journey had she not been a hero as a little girl—and as a victim.

She was also eloquently described in Robert Coles' book, *The Moral Life of Children*, and other places because she was one of the children he interviewed and followed during his work as a social psychologist. She had a moral strength within that enabled her to

do what was important for many others. I think Rockwell would
have tackled the challenging topic of the victims of homophobic
bigotry had he lived longer, perhaps finding an equivalent for Ruby
Bridges.

Ignorance is a challenging foe. But it is more easily confronted
when it is open than when it is cloaked behind something that is
legitimate like freedom of speech. In the long run ignorance is best
destroyed when it is attacked from within rather than externally.

I sometimes use the image of putting a thumbtack into Jello
to attach that colorful substance to the wall to illustrate the difficulty
of pinning down some problems. If the three seniors cannot see
the ignorance of their ways they will continue with them forever.
Because of their use of a public forum and the outcry it generated,
they now have to deal with their beliefs by learning more facts
(pedophile stats), by seeing people as individuals for who they are,
by examining the categorization and labeling they have been
practicing. They are not alone, they will not be the last, and there
will be more people with hurt feelings, anger, and fear before we
reach Utopia (which literally means "nowhere"). Yet the boys may
also hold firm to the committed faith in their beliefs and not
understand why those that practice and support the homosexual
"lifestyle" will not see the ignorance of that way. The middle ground
of either/or is . . . ?

Sexuality is not a comfortable topic for most people. It easily
becomes personalized, and public discussion of one's sexual
preferences and practices is not going to attract a diverse crowd—
at least for long. And yet it is the most widely sought after topic on
the Internet: for the most part it is called pornography. In the
privacy of our computer anyone of us can vicariously experience
any form of sexual expression. Apparently, many of our youth in
particular do. After alcohol, the leading reason for students failing
out of college is the Internet, and I would suspect that pornographic
surfing is one of the factors in that method of spending time.

How much better would we all be, as individuals and as a
society, if teenagers could examine sexuality in a safe and open
environment? I know moving in such a direction in education is

not favored by many Americans, perhaps most. That discussion, many argue, belongs in the family and not in the school, with individual guidance and not with community involvement. The United States had a surgeon general resign because she talked frankly about masturbation. But the reality is that most parents are not comfortable talking about sexuality with their children, because it opens the door to a personal discussion of the parents' own sexuality. All of us exercise a measure of personal censorship. "It's none of your business!"

But doesn't personal "business" affect other people? It certainly did with Bill Clinton; but he was acting as the President of the United States, a role he could not take a vacation from. No parent can ever take a vacation from being a parent. I guess the Dean could take a vacation from school, but he better not be "caught" doing something shameful during personal time. It would embarrass the village as well as himself. Bill Clinton hurt many people by his actions, but he was certainly scrutinized on a regular basis to a degree that few of us would enjoy. We do not want that kind of attention.

Neither does the teenager concerned about his or her sexual identity.

I am not trained to counsel kids about sexual identity concerns. I am eager, however, to direct them to someone who is. Yet what is the ratio in our schools of experienced counselors to kids? Every teenager needs guidance, even though every one does not need counseling. How many adults are comfortable giving that guidance? I oversaw 460 kids at the beginning of this school year. If 2% of them were homosexual, that's only nine students. If 10% were struggling with sexual identity that would be 45. If 50% were struggling with sexuality in general (the raging hormone syndrome), that's 230. And of the worrisome triumvirate that emerged from the turbulent '60's—sex, drugs, and rock and roll—sex may be the most important, but it is clearly not the only problem we worry about.

I do not have the solution. I do have some strategies and ideas that will work sometimes for me and also for my school. But I have no doubt that more people need to strategize and work on these problems, to train even more people to help as the next group of kids come along, and to know that each long journey starts with a single step.

One step I tried was to offer my services to the student body one evening to have an open forum to talk about sexuality. There was an impetus to this particular forum. We recently had had a dance, and it was quite successful. Attendance was strong, kids had a good time, and there was no obvious drug and alcohol use.

For any who have watched television, and more specifically that vanguard of pop culture—MTV—you know that dancing is even more blatantly sexual than Elvis's thrusting with his pelvis two generations ago. Seeing it on television is not quite the same as seeing your own students live and in action. Several of the chaperones at this particular dance reported their concern, or discomfort, or disgust, or any combination of these feelings. I asked them to give me some names, and I announced in assembly and through the email system that I would like to hold an open discussion about the issues. No prejudgments, no disciplinary actions to follow; just a discussion. I invited about ten kids specifically.

Over 25 showed up to this after-dinner meeting, including one of the chaperones and the assistant Dean and myself. The rules were that everyone had to speak only when called on (I kept a running list of who wanted to speak), and that everyone had to listen to what others had to say. We talked for an hour. People came after we started, people left before we finished, some talked several times, and some not at all. There were seniors and freshman, girls and boys, white kids and non-white kids. Several people emailed apologies about having another commitment and were sorry they could not attend.

What was significant was the eagerness and willingness of kids to talk and have adults be part of the audience and part of the discussion. Kids want this kind of forum, and they want guidance and openness to explore issues. But they want to be listened to, not preached at.

One question raised, and not just by the adults, was: would you dance like this (including what is euphemistically called "lapdancing" as well as the vertical equivalent), if your parents or grandparents were present? For most, the answer was "no," while for some it was "yes". Another question was whether this was the physical expression of dance or more of a sexual activity. Again, a variety of opinions.

The challenge here was to agree to disagree. That is not easy, and not everyone subscribes to that view. If something is "wrong" then we should not tolerate disagreement.

While the issue of homosexuality was not discussed, at some point I would hope it could be in such a context. That would be far more uncomfortable, and agreeing to disagree would be less acceptable. But how else can we get the tough topics on the table for kids? Institutions, in general, cannot and/or will not take on the task; individuals do not always have the cachet to draw in a large and diverse group or the comfort level to lead a discussion if assigned by the institution to participate.

I tried a second forum several weeks later, this one on racial profiling. Almost as many kids came, but I was the only adult, which was ok because sometimes teenagers are simply intimidated by too many members of the authority structure. Nevertheless, we had a good discussion.

And then I went on sabbatical. I itched to do more forums, wanted kids to have more open discussions about the tough topics, hoped perhaps even the kids themselves would organize forums. Perhaps it will happen. The school is still addressing the issue of homophobia as a result of the newspaper letter and articles. But as a school, a village, a country, a world, we have to have those discussions.

The issue of homophobia has been in the student newspaper well before my time as Dean starting in the fall of 1992. There have been articles every year since then, sometimes editorials, sometimes letters, sometimes articles about events that discussed the concern. Some have been antagonistic towards the gay "lifestyle," some have been more focused on the need for tolerance and acceptance. There is no consensus on the topic.

Schools, and especially those that are more independent (a class of institutions that are not run directly by the local communities and the state, as they are in public schools), can have speakers and meetings where everyone has to attend. They can then have smaller meetings to follow up, to enable students to talk further about the topic of the meeting. They can more easily tackle topics like homosexuality and homophobia. Yet there is still a risk of offending powerful people who might even go so far as withdraw their support of the school or withdraw their student from the school.

I don't know that we have prevented any suicides or more violent attacks against homosexuals because we have taken some institutional steps to address our concerns. I do know that individuals have sought counseling because of our leadership. I count that as positive.

We have had assemblies with individual speakers (a gay Republican leader in Massachusetts), forums (GLSTN: Gay, Lesbian, Straight Teachers Network), and performers (The Flirtations, an *a cappella* gay singing group). We have had faculty professional days with speakers and workshops. We have had former students who are now openly gay return to talk with groups of interested students.

While that is too much for some (anything on the topic would be too much for a few), it is not enough for most.

The Flirtations performance was a good example.

Jon Arterton taught here for seven years before moving on to do an MFA, become more involved with performance, and eventually struggle through some difficult personal issues that resulted in him coming out of the closet and accepting his gayness. He eventually formed the Flirtations, performing on the street corners of New York, later in concerts, even in the movie *Philadelphia*.

Jon and I were good friends from the first year we began as teachers. We had many adventures together, threw an annual bash for several years to thank our many married friends who had included us in social activities, performed together in a school production of Hamlet, and generally, together with several others, "hung out." Life was good, but we both moved on. Soon he dropped his connections with his former friends here. He virtually disappeared into the inner life of New York. He had come out of the closet there, but he decided to sever his ties with part of his past.

Through some investigation, persistence, and initiative several of us found him again, and we met for lunch in New York City. He announced he was gay. There were three of us adults, my friends Ellis and Barbara Baker and I, and their two pre-teen daughters, and Jon. We all nodded, said So? And our friendship was reestablished.

Jon and his Flirtations showed up at my wedding several years later because they were doing a concert in a neighboring city. They sang several terrific songs. I was proud they had participated.

A couple of years later I inquired if they would perform at an assembly and use it as a forum to discuss homosexual issues. They thought it was a great opportunity and scheduled a date. They performed on March 30, 1994. I thought they were terrific; but, then again, I was biased. The ovation was another piece of evidence, individual discussions with a number of students was yet another.

The Flirtations were not only an outstanding musical group; they were politically involved. They did not just sing songs; they sent a message. They also talked about themselves as individuals, relating personal stories that revealed they had achievements, heartbreaks, love, and failure—just like everyone else. Jon had been a cross-country runner in college, had coached the wrestling team at my school, had taught English, had seen his former girlfriend die of AIDS as a result of a blood transfusion.

But they also were not "just like anyone else"

They performed spectacularly, and then they answered questions for anyone who had them. The students were not shy, and the Flirtations were well versed in the personal, social, and religious contexts of the questions asked. It was an excellent dialogue.

The assembly also led to a direct confrontation between a

couple of students and their parents who did not think they should have to attend an assembly that was led by openly gay—thus immoral—people. They wanted to be excused and not have to accrue a consequence (an unexcused absence), for missing the required assembly. They even confronted the Headmaster directly to protest the performance.

They were a minority, not alone, but a minority. They survived the experience, the school community benefited far more, and discussion continued. The four performers of The Flirtations had individually suffered more severely in their lifetimes than most of our students had and likely the adults, and they had made an impact on the lives of others.

If the homophobes in our society could perform with the same sense of dignity that this particular group of homosexuals did that day, then there would be a chance of dialogue. Yet it does seem difficult to mix dignity with hate, disgust, or contempt. Dignity and homophobia are simply not going to reside in the same room. One will have to leave.

CENSOR IT—OR NOT?

I was asked informally to sit in on a class this winter to be an "expert" witness for the defense in a debate as to whether the library should be subscribing to *Rolling Stone* magazine. The prosecution contended it was obscene, pornographic, and inappropriate for students at the school. While the older student may be able to contend with such material, the prosecution argued, they were concerned for younger students and even faculty children who may see such material, and then presumably look at it.

The defense focused on the First amendment, the concerns for censorship, and the freedom of choice. In hindsight I am not quite sure why I was asked to be part of the presentation. A student asked me my opinions and then felt the weight of the Dean would carry the argument to the jury, her peers. I presume that if I had not been on her side philosophically she would have thanked me and not asked me to attend.

The whole process was well researched by the class, sound arguments were presented articulately by both sides, questions and cross examinations were carried on in a formal and considered fashion.

The defense lost 5-2. Of course, I was stunned! I found the overall sentiment interesting, and probably different from what it would have been ten years earlier, and perhaps different from what it might have been if the students were seniors rather than sophomores. More students now seem to want a less contentious atmosphere in the community. One way to achieve that would be to prevent or exorcise the offending dissonance.

While the mainstream of American culture seems to be spending an inordinate amount of time and money on MTV and its relatives and what they are sponsoring, this group of students objected to the prurient nature of the magazine's content. They did not want to ignore it or walk away from it; they wanted to ban it. Some of the prosecutors had a replacement magazine all lined up.

I find it interesting that I did not title one of my chapters SEX; after all sex sells. And certainly sex is on the minds of the hormonally charged teenagers, and it is clearly manifested in dress and behavior. Most of us adults wish it would just go away; we were uncomfortable with it when we were teenagers, and now we all know better and cannot understand why these kids today just don't get it! I think the teenage response is: As if! In the warm weather sex pervades our society with how we dress. In the cold weather it is mostly on TV. Mostly in our village, but not always, the concern is about the teenagers. I am never sure whether the girls are naïve or deliberately provocative, and we struggle and battle over warm weather attire. The Dress Code states:

> "Appropriate academic day dress includes shirts and dress t-shirts with collars, sleeves, or buttons. Shirts may be worn un-tucked. Shirts may not have print of any kind, but they may have stitching if appropriate. No more than two buttons from the top of a shirt may be unbuttoned. Shirts must have a modest cut neckline. Dresses, like shirts, must have collars, sleeves or buttons. Skirts, dresses, and shorts must be at least mid-thigh in length . . . and no underwear or bare midriffs may be showing."

I hope the reader can envision a group including adults and teenagers trying to reach consensus on such a statement! Related to this issue are body piercings, tattoos, and hair dye. These are fads that come and go, challenging the authorities along the way and giving grist for the psychologists and sociologists. Some schools react by banning or somehow regulating these activities. We do not ban or regulate them as of now. I don't foresee us doing anything in the immediate future either. I think the dress code is challenging and distracting enough. Here again, these appearance issues might be symbolic of something serious or just normal teenage experimentation. They can be dangerous (blood poisoning), or they might just be embarrassing (hair color), to some of the authorities. They might signal depression or alienation.

Some would say that sexuality has nothing to do with any of this, that it is style, personal right, taste, etc. Some would have a stronger set of rules; we call them the Taliban. Some would have no rules; we call them liberated (?). It is an interesting battle, certainly not new as we look back through concerns people had in different times in American history. I am not convinced it is a battle that can be won or lost, but certainly there will be casualties along the way. Some are personal casualties as teenagers give and receive feedback about their dress. Some are institutional casualties as schools, at least the private ones, vie for acceptance by applicants and their parents who place more or less emphasis on appearance.

Most adults are not especially comfortable talking about sexuality with teenagers, especially with their own children. The result is that discussions are among peer groups, and the greatest influence is from the media. Parents and educators straggle at the end of the line.

How important is our personal sexuality to our self-esteem? Apparently to teenagers it ranks pretty high. For some it seems not to rank particularly high, and those kids seem to be emotionally healthier. Note all this unscientific observation from the Dean. I work in a school that has a pretty wide range of teenagers: those that are repressed, those that are liberated, those that peers call sluts, those that other peers call studs, those that are comfortable with themselves at least on the surface, those that may be struggling with sexual identity and orientation. I have talked to individuals of each gender, groups of each gender, groups with both genders. And every year there will be a new group at each age. The good talk with the fourteen year old does not mean that there will not have to be other talks the next year or three years later.

Teens do not get sick, pregnant, emotionally shattered, or socially devastated by doing poorly in an academic class. However, sexual angst and/or activity can certainly have serious consequences.

I need to qualify the last two in that list of difficulties because from time to time there is an individual who can have that level of distress by doing poorly in or failing an academic class. I suspect self-esteem issues in that case are also on an end of the bell curve. The other factor with academic performance is parental expectation and the pressure it engenders. A number of years ago a Head read a letter to the faculty at the beginning of the school year which included the statement that "failure was not an option" for his child. The Head countered with the point that failure is always an option; it just was not an attractive one or an acceptable for the parent's set of expectations. The consequences were unthinkable. For the school? The student? Failure would certainly have to be somebody's fault. Fortunately, the student did fine so we did not have to learn what the consequences of an unacceptable situation would be.

And yet I think that failure in social situations that revolve around sexuality disconcert if not devastate more of our teenagers than academic shortcomings. The report cards are just not officially filed.

Adults are different from teenagers. The rules are different, and they should be. The workplace and the social place are also different, and they should be. Yet we all know that the lines get blurred in the adult community plenty of times, and the consequences are sometimes just as destructive as they are for the teens. But teenagers should not have the same responsibility for those consequences. I hope I am being authoritative rather than authoritarian in that sentiment.

Eighteen year olds are adults in many categories, but in schools not all those categories apply. No eighteen year old has to stay in school, and thus by agreeing to remain, the teenager accepts more constrictions than if he or she were not in school. While we might understand that the eighteen year old may be ready for an active sexual life, we (or at least I and all those that agree), would not accept the same liberty for fourteen year olds. The younger ones simply are not emotionally prepared, the physical appearance and reality notwithstanding. Now we are not going to ban mini skirts for freshmen and allow them for seniors; it is the same school. In school we think such attire is inappropriate during the class day; we may also feel it is inappropriate the rest of the time as well, but I think we then become involved in personal rather than institutional relationships with kids. For the most part, parents are supportive of our dress code during the school day as far as the rules and philosophy apply; after that time the alliance unravels, partly for simple practicality. The school is not an island, and our students are not confined. Other schools may have more success with the dress code issue, and I speak only for my own situation. I also see the media; so do all the kids.

The school newspaper is not a free press. Free speech does not mean consequences do not follow. People in authority are gatekeepers, and there are occasions when the gate must be closed. This applies to dress, behavior, publications and even whether a student can remain in the school. Yes, there is and should be some censorship. We just do not all agree where the line should be drawn.

THE INCENTIVE FACTOR

One of the wonderful things we see in a community is the good that people do. Those events of altruism or basic good nature do not always stick out, and we have too much of an interest in the problems we encounter. Nevertheless, the incidents that confirm an optimistic view of our teenagers are always worth noting.

Sometimes the actions are the result of an idea that several people have, but those actions coming to reality usually reflect the efforts of one or two people. An example at our school was the creation of the Big Brother/ Big/Sister program. Certainly this was not an innovation, but it was an introduction to our school. We may ask why it took so long, but I would rather focus on the fact that it came into being and give some credit to the students who made it happen. A number of people were involved, but it was a student's initiative, and she energized enough other people to make it happen. The program seems now as though it is a normal tradition—even though it is only in its third year.

This particular student had been to our school as a commuting middle school student, transferred to a more prestigious boarding school and then returned after some unhappiness and more trouble than I think we knew about. The other school had the tradition of the Big/Brother Big/Sister program and she wanted to adapt it. As she was reintegrating to our school, she began to push for this program. Her persistence infected other students and adults, a preliminary process began in the spring, and in the fall of her senior year it was under way.

Seeing students give up their "free" time on a Sunday afternoon for several hours to mentor these younger kids signified both an individual and community commitment to what nationally has been emphasized as volunteerism. Only a few students are actually involved in the program, but it is visible, praiseworthy, and sustained. As a result of an individual's initiative and whatever internal incentive this girl had, the program works.

Perhaps it was this effort on her part, perhaps it was the good feeling she derived from it, perhaps it was simply the maturation process taking hold; whatever her motivation, she was a significantly different factor in our community than she was when she first re-arrived at our school. She was not a different person; she was not "fixed" by our program or our efforts to encourage and assist her in following her chosen path. She simply had emerged from a tumultuous period in her teen years, but her solid foundation for becoming a successful adult had been set many years before she ever entered our little community.

Another interesting and visible success story of incentive was the establishment of a program called the Heifer project. The goal of this project, an international-based organization, is to raise $5000 to provide the means of sustenance for a community: an ark of animals to help them learn to become self-reliant rather than dependant on outside resources. Here again, the initiative came from a small group of students, and they successfully promoted the idea in a school-wide fashion. They, and the rest of the school, were indeed proud when they accepted a mock-copy of the check and a plaque signifying their achievement.

While the core of kids actively moving this project was small, their infectious commitment moved everyone else. Only in a village where there can be this combination of personal commitment with community support does such success occur. People must know other people, must be communicative with other people, and must feel that their initiative will be supported. They must have a sense of involvement beyond themselves and their immediate friends. It does not happen everywhere.

Not all such efforts need to be so ennobling. Some are just group activities: the establishment of a Frisbee program, a somewhat offbeat game of medieval battle where students chased each other around with padded lances, an activities program that encouraged students to initiate events they wanted. I came across a group of students playing cards one day. I grew up with cards, whiling away hours as a youth playing a variety of solitaire games, cribbage early on with my father, different games with other friends, hearts and Michigan rummy at prep school, bridge in college. When I saw these kids playing cards I selfishly encouraged them to play bridge, a game several of them actually knew how to play. We established a bridge club for a couple of years, and I would sneak away to the Student Center during an Activities period once a week to get in a couple of hands. We had a good time, and eventually this small core had enough for two tables on occasion. Alas, several graduated the same year and the tradition died.

I think this kind of activity happens frequently, and I took a small measure of pride in being welcomed into a group of teenagers for their game. I know one went off to college and became involved in a bridge group there. It happened to be my alma mater. I added to my own sense of self-esteem by sending forth a graduate into the next academic world with an interest beyond books and classes.

Each of these examples has nothing to do with me as the Dean. What they do reflect, however, is the more generic examples of villages or communities that can engender success stemming from a secondary tier of leaders. It is not always the adults that do the leading in a school. Strong leadership from both students and adults produces a cohesive community that is dynamic. While there will continue to be tension between students and adults in a school, and there should be, when there is communication and even partnership the school acts much more as a community.

The internal incentive for students to become proctors is sometimes hard to identify. Some like the idea of power, some like the possibility of a single room, some want to pass on lessons that they learned from others, some want to beef up their college application portfolio, some genuinely want to make a contribution to the school. Proctors in the dormitories are a natural fit because they live among the students, live in a building that serves as home and houses an extended family of faculty and students. The role of proctors among the commuting student population was more difficult to define, but we instituted it anyway. I take responsibility for instituting that new role for students, but it remains a bit of a group without an easily defined sense of purpose. My hope was to establish some leadership with that group, to incorporate those students further into the life of the school, and to have them take on more responsibility in making our community work better. Of course, they wanted to know what their privileges could be, otherwise why bother to do it! Gradually we have more students who want to be part of making the community a better place. I then have a defined group of students who I can utilize as a sounding board, and also can utilize to resolve problems. Many of them have been as concerned as some of the adults about behaviors in the student center, or with cars, or with interpersonal relationships. Now they feel as though they have a role in making both place and people more welcoming for everyone. We continue to talk about privileges—can the proctors park at the gym; can they clear Units; can they give Units!—but they understand that those discussions should really be secondary. It is not a particularly formal group, not a high profile group, but there are ten or twelve more juniors and seniors who have a stake in the village.

THE MODEL

Freshman boys are small anyway, and this one was only a little larger than the average. He was a good athlete, confident enough as a person that boarding school would not present him with insurmountable challenges. He hoped to make the varsity basketball team, but he knew that was probably not going to happen that year. He and his roommate, who played hockey, were compatible if not best friends.

He had a successful freshman year, played JV basketball, made Honors in the second semester, had many friends. One of his best friends in the dorm left school after the first semester, unhappy with himself as well as unsuccessful in the classroom. His friend had failed one course, barely passed two others, and was placed on Academic Probation. He also had started smoking marijuana fairly regularly but had not been caught. His parents were in the middle of a divorce, and he was simply unhappy being away from home.

Seeing that friend leave school had an impact on the boy, causing him to reflect on what he had, perhaps motivating him to work a little harder in his studies, leading him to have an Honors average.

He had plenty of learning experiences that freshman year. He watched one of the junior proctors exercise authority in a way that demonstrated more concern for power than responsibility. He was tangentially involved in what could have been termed harassment of one of the smaller boys in the dorm. He saw one of his friends throw a snowball at a passing car and end up on Probation because the driver called the school. The Dean had tracked down the guilty party. But the freshman had many more positive experiences than negative ones.

For his sophomore year he wanted to move to one of the bigger dorms in the center of campus, and he and another boy decided to room together. Sophomore year was easier academically than the freshman year because he had learned how to study, and there were enough new sophomores to the school that the teachers sometimes had to slow the pace to allow the new students to learn techniques he had learned the year before.

He did not grow much, and he did not make the varsity basketball team again, but he had learned lacrosse as a freshman and he became much more interested in that sport. He began to feel he had more of a future as a varsity player there; older and more talented basketball players arrived on campus as new juniors or post-graduate players.

In February his roommate bought a bottle of vodka and invited several students to his room to party. The boy was there when a dorm parent knocked on the door. The alcohol was discovered, and an investigation ensued. The boy had to go to the Discipline Committee because he wanted to contest that he should be placed on Probation for the "in the presence of" rule. The school rule said that students in the presence of an illegal activity would be subject to Probation the same as someone who was an active participant.

The Committee accepted the defense that he had not been drinking, but they placed him on Probation because it was his responsibility to leave that situation. He had voluntarily remained to socialize. While his roommate was suspended for a week, had to have an evaluation for substance use, and had to sign a no-use contract and accept random drug screening, he was given only Probation and a week of room confinement. He knew he had been wrong and he accepted his punishment without rancor.

One other positive outcome was a healthy and open conversation with his parents. While they were disappointed, they also recognized that he had been placed in an awkward situation and in fact had made a good decision not to imbibe. They hoped the lesson would not be forgotten.

Being on Probation until the start of the next year made him ineligible to become a proctor until the new year, but he was not sure he was ready for that step anyway. In a dorm with sophomores, juniors and seniors—some of whom were postgraduates—being a junior proctor was a serious challenge. He could wait.

As a junior, he knew the academic commitments would be considerably greater, and he had gotten into the AP section of US History. With Physics, Algebra II Honors, Spanish III, and all the reading for English he would be working hard. He stayed in the same dorm again. He had the opportunity to move to another dorm and get a single room, but he opted to stay with his friends and in the center of campus.

By the end of the year two of his friends had left school for disciplinary reasons, but he had stayed clear of difficulties. It was not necessarily that he kept troubled company, but rather that he was friendly with many students. He remained focused academically, decided to try squash for his winter sport rather than continue with basketball, lettered on the varsity because his athletic ability and work ethic gave him an edge in a sport that was not mainstream at his school. He also started writing for the newspaper and was persuaded to try for the *a cappella* singing group where he made the cut. He was busy.

He lettered in lacrosse, was elected captain for his senior year, and won the Most Improved Player Award. Finally, he applied for proctorship and was selected, choosing a single in the same dorm rather than sharing a suite with another student. He knew he would value the opportunity to have some time for himself.

In the senior year, he felt overwhelmed for much of the first semester, finally opting not to apply Early Decision to college. He met a girl, started dating steadily, helped a junior boy get to Health Services because he had an alcohol problem, saw two seniors leave before graduation for disciplinary reasons, and helped mediate a difficult situation between a new teacher and his obstreperous seniors in an English class. He earned two more varsity letters, a citation for his English research paper, and a citizenship award at graduation.

After the graduation ceremony he cried freely. He had not fully realized how hard it would be to say good-bye to a life that had been all encompassing. But he also knew he had move on. He would do so, well prepared in many areas.

THE POLITICS OF
THE VILLAGE

Perhaps since Watergate the reputation of politicians and politics in general has drifted downward, not helped in the least by the events of the 1990's. While Bill Clinton did very well in polls as President and exercised strong leadership (according to some), he did not help the mood of the country with his personal behavior. Nor did his detractors, those who were out to "get him," do the country service by their own behaviors. While criticism of personal behavior has almost always been the stuff of politics, it became more salacious in the 1990's, more personally intimate, less relevant—perhaps sometimes not relevant at all—to the governance of the nation.

Politics refers to the decisions made that are pertinent to the society as a whole, the "body politic." Decisions are not made irrespective of the society as a whole. Decisions do not just affect an individual or a small group. The ripple effect is stronger or less so depending on the nature of the incident or the decision. The same is true in schools or in villages. The concept of the six degrees of separation—that any individual can be connected to any other individual on the planet by a maximum of five other people—is reduced dramatically in a village or a school. If a student does something unacceptable, the disciplinary result will affect everyone else pretty quickly. The politics of the situation, however, recognize what those effects will be before the decision is made.

Cynics will conclude that politics are the primary reason for any decision, moralists will decide strictly on right versus wrong regardless of the ripple effect. I would prefer neither be in power.

Do we have a different standard for the student who is the

quarterback, the lead in the play, or the child of a wealthy donor than for the student who is none of those? Strictly speaking I hope not, but does a student's contribution to the community weigh in when deciding whether that individual should be dismissed from school or given one more chance, another—in the parlance of some critics—"a double secret Probation?" I think the answer should be a qualified yes.

When someone has to appear before the Discipline Committee to receive a recommendation allowing that person to remain, those political factors come into play. So do they when the recommendation sits in front of the Headmaster, the final adjudicator. Serving on the Discipline Committee or sitting in the Headmaster's chair requires both wisdom and strength. Someone is going to be less than satisfied with the decision.

> "{You son]'s incident with alcohol last Friday night placed him in jeopardy of dismissal from the . . . School. Following my letter for his Probation for being out of the dorm after check-in only several weeks ago, this incident was most discouraging. However, at his Discipline Committee hearing, [he] presented a case for being allowed to either continue or return . . . rather than be dismissed outright. He admitted that he was under stress for several reasons and that he was genuinely sorry and disappointed in himself for his lapse of judgment.

> "The sentiment on the Committee was not unanimous, partly because [he] admitted that he was largely responsible for the purchase of the alcohol and that he had intended to get drunk prior to going to [town].

> The disposition was that [he] would be separated for the remainder of the year and allowed to petition to return following successful academic work for the rest of the year and successful efforts to address his problems with alcohol and other underlying issues. When [he] has worked on these

issues and feels, with your support, that he would like to
petition the Headmaster for reinstatement, he should write
a detailed letter with supporting evidence from a counselor/
therapist who has expertise in areas of alcohol and family
counseling. Consultation with our Health Services personnel
about the process before the summer begins would also be
important.

While there should not be an automatic presumption
that [he] will in fact be successful in his petition, he at least
does have that option."

Several people, including both adults and students, spoke on
the student's behalf at the Committee hearing, citing positive
contributions he had made. Some members of the Committee felt
he was worth having another chance, while others did not. I knew
of issues that he was confronting separately in Health Services.
The Headmaster decided to support the risk of allowing him to
return. The boy reenrolled over the summer and graduated the
following year.

A senior, boarding for four years, had two incidents in his last
year after having none for three years. He had lied at Health Services
about missing a commitment and then later had plagiarized a paper
by downloading information from the Internet. He was also one
Unit shy of yet another Probation. He was a proctor, a varsity
athlete, and a well-liked student by peers and adults alike. After
his second incident, the Committee recommended that he be
Separated until graduation but allowed to participate in the
ceremony and receive his diploma. They struggled with the
inconsistency of retaining someone who made two errors in one
year, with a third one imminent, but they felt he deserved
something other than Dismissal. The Committee found a creative
solution.

The following is an excerpt from a lengthy letter to the
President of the Board of Trustees from a parent whose son was
dismissed. He had been involved in an alcohol incident and then

persisted in lying. He had also been on Probation the previous year for possession of an empty bottle of wine. The politics of the decision in this case had far less to do with the individual or the family than they did with the severity of the case. Nevertheless, in the middle of the letter there was a statement about one aspect of politics:

> "*when my husband told [the Head] that there may be a need to write to the Board of Trustees and to the . . . Board for Private Schools about the handling of this matter, the Head said, to this effect, 'then I have no alternative. I will not help your son in finding a place in another school.' This is a case of blatant blackmail, and I am sure that if we take it up with our lawyer, we have cause for a legal case.*"

The letter included a summary from the parent's perspective about the events that had transpired.

> "*. . . a friend approached my son and asked him if he'd go along with a couple of other guys . . . to buy beer. He willingly agreed to go. He did not call for the taxi, he did not go into the liquor store, he does not possess an illegal ID, he did not purchase the beer, he did not take possession of the beer, he did not drink the beer. Yes, he did go and yes, he did give the 'friend' his bag in which to hide the liquor while bringing it back to campus. Yes, he did deny that the bag was his when confronted with it. After the cab driver, rightfully so, reported the incident to the administration at [the school], an investigation was started [One boy] came to [my son] and the other two boys involved and begged them to cover up the whole affair. Once again, they all agreed and concocted a story that would be their cover story. My son wrote it down and another from the group photocopied it and gave each one a copy to make sure they would keep the story straight.*
> *During the following 2 weeks the boys were questioned on and off about the affair. A while later, [the first boy] went, on*

his own, to admit the entire affair. That afternoon, when my son and [his friend] found out that [one boy] had told the true story, they tried to see Dean Swanson to confess also. He told them he was too busy to meet with them. When called in front of the disciplinary board, my son said he DID at that point present the true account of events."

Several pages later there was a list of thirteen points. The first nine were directed towards the Head and the Assistant Head, but they did not apply to me directly.

10. *It has been alleged that Dean Swanson lied to [a student] by telling him that the beer was found in [another student's] room rather than in the storage area as he knew it was. [He] actually confronted Dean Swanson with this allegation, and told him that he had lied about it to [the boy]. It appears that not only did a member of the discipline committee engage in duplicity, just as the 4 students did, but did it for the purpose of entrapment. Lying is lying, and if this allegation is true, then Dean Swanson makes a travesty of the whole discipline committee and what it stands for. [The Head] had told me directly that it wasn't the beer run that got our son expelled, but rather the lying about it. How can the school justify lying on the part of a committee member who expelled our son for doing the exact same thing?*

11. *[The school] professes, in its handbook, to be a nurturing school sensitive to the feelings of its students. I find the manner in which this whole affair was conducted humiliating and manipulated. To have to move out in front of an audience and be made a spectacle in front of students and parents speaks of the callousness and insensitivity of the administration. The fact alone that the school waited until Parents' Day to give us the information without even a hint as to the existence of the*

crisis pending shows a total lack of any empathy or basic
consideration on the part of administration. Whatever
[our son] did does not justify the insensitivity of the
administration in dealing [his] father, a parent.

12. As a gesture of good faith on our part, we paid last year's
and this year's tuition in full in August . . . , plus donated
$500 to the annual fund after our son was in the school for
only 6 months. We were delighted with his enthusiasm
and love of [the school], and we were also delighted at his
personal, social, and academic growth. Because we feel
that this situation does not merit the severity of an expulsion,
we feel cheated out of the $20,000 we had paid in advance.
Had [he] done something to merit an expulsion, we would
feel differently.

13. [Another student's] father stated to my husband that he
knows things are getting out of control in the school and
the administration had to take an action to show the
students that they are in control. He himself said that the
punishment meted out to [our son] was too severe for his
involvement in the beer run incident.

In the one year in which our son has been at your school, a
number of other 'dangerous' or irregular situations have
occurred. Since [the Head and Assistant Head] are
vigorously attempting to ensure and preserve the integrity
of the students and the reputation of the school, let me
briefly list the incidents about which I have been told. If
these are indeed true, they merit action. If they are fabricated,
then at the very least they should be clarified to erase the
image they are casting upon the school.

1. In October, . . . , 2 girls came back to their dorm DRUNK
and a senior administrative officer "spoke" to them. They
remained on campus.

2. *—A student on 3rd probation was found with 'weapons'
    (bat, knife, chains). He remains on campus.*

3. *A student signed out for Boston one weekend, then went to
    [a local town], rented a motel room and threw a drinking
    party for the weekend. He remains on campus.*

4. *. . . the owner and user of the false ID, who purchased the
    beer, begged the other 3 students to stick together on a story
    which would protect him, and then, ALONE went to
    relate the true story, remains on campus.*

5. *A student, . . . , was expelled last year. When asked how
    he got reinstated, he told our son that his parents wrote
    letters to the school and gave a DONATION. He was
    reinstated.*

6. *One of the students on the discipline committee is on his
    3rd probation.*

7. *Drug use on campus is not uncommon.*

One underlying consideration was also economic, not just the
tuition but also the reference to the donation to the annual fund.
I am not sure whether that was meant to be a consideration for the
Head and the Board.

> *"If the inappropriate and inconsistent actions reported have
> occurred as reported, we feel you will find with us that a refund
> of the tuition for the remainder of the school year is an
> appropriate request despite the policy on refunds. The school
> erred, the damage done to our son cannot be repaired, and
> apologies from school officials who acted inappropriately are not
> sought. But the money can, and we feel should be, refunded and
> we therefore request it by the end of January."*

A long letter with numerous allegations! As a school and as individuals we survived the crisis, which included the incident and student cover-up and then the parental reaction. I confidently feel there was untruth and misinformation included in the letter, and in the end three of the four boys left the school. I had made notes on a daily basis for two weeks prior to the final confessions and disciplinary committee response. This case was not one that was hastily developed.

These particular parents did not reside in the United States and thus communication was by fax and telephone. I am not sure their son ever did confess to them his complete role in the events. Although he eventually gave them some truth, they were determined to have a review. His truth was not the truth as I saw it. The parents did recognize that their son did at least lie and cover-up for two weeks, and I and others believed further that he continued to lie about his full participation in the events. The Board of Trustees apparently felt the process and decision were appropriate. I heard nothing further.

The politics of the events ended in the result that there were no extenuating circumstances that would warrant less than Dismissal. The words "blackmail" and "donation" in the letter along with other allegations implied that others had received special consideration that was not afforded to this boy. While there were undoubtedly more conferences that I was not party to as the Dean, I doubt that there was successful political lobbying or pressure that unduly influenced anyone at the school. The boy deserved to be dismissed, and he was.

Second-guessing is an age-old practice. It has been successfully co-opted by sports enthusiasts so that it is now in our daily lexicon: Monday morning quarterbacking. It is related to that popular exercise: What if? And it all takes place after the fact. We have allowed several students to return rather than be dismissed, only to fail again. That does not always mean we made the wrong decision.

Political considerations do play a role in the village or the

school. In some ways these are more insidious than in the wider
world because there is no place to hide. We often use the fishbowl
analogy. We are self-consciously uncomfortable with the pressures
that accompany living among the people we work with. The politics
is more muted than in the American society as a whole because
one has to face, literally, the accuser or denouncer. In the larger
society, commentators can hurl epithets and accusations from afar,
personally unseen though known by by-line, or radio voice, or
television. It is easier to sling mud—an old-fashioned American
term—and then move on to the next issue without having to
apologize or be held accountable by the community.

Nevertheless, in my school we have had our normal share of
tendentious issues, sometimes personalized to a discomforting
degree. They have included personal attacks on individuals,
nefarious comparisons of one group to another, and hurtful diatribes
that focused on a particular group. Discipline decisions have often
released angry responses by both faculty members and students.
Decisions within the adult community about salary, workload, or
housing have elicited comments that have not always been helpful.

There are political pressures brought to bear on individuals by
other individuals or constituencies. Some of the quoted letters I
have cited represent this pressure. The Head of the school suffers
these kinds of pressures frequently. The Director of Admissions
also receives them. Recall the mother who told me to drop dead;
her son was a late admittance at the specific plea of a trustee. I have
had phone calls as well from trustees, inquiring about why an
individual student was dismissed from school because the parents
have asked the trustee to intervene. Invariably, the parents have
not told the whole story or have not had the perspective of the
Dean or the school in reference to the issue. One trustee did resign
because of his son's dismissal, but I think that had more to do with
his own personal issues in struggling with his son's difficulties.

We make decisions on political considerations. If the result of
the consideration would do more harm to the community—e.g.,
retain a particular student who has influence—then it would be
unwise to retain the student. But if we think the benefit to both

the individual and the community is greater by keeping the student then a by-the-books decision is tempered. Pundits and critics are not going to like that; it is based on judgment rather than a fixed standard. This is not to imply there are no standards; there are. They are just not absolute.

And yet despite all of these difficulties, I would be hard-pressed to find anyone who would think the school is not better than it was ten years ago. The flows have been stronger and more consistent than the ebbs. Our rules are tighter; our students are better behaved, more focused; our faculty is more committed.

It is no doubt too soon to be making definitive statements about almost anything in the last decade, but most of the "poor" decisions were either rectified or resolved to the good in the long run. The "long run" is not finished. I can only conclude that much has been going better and that none of us should get too comfortable.

We take chances on kids, not poor risks but reasonable risks. There are risks for gain and risks for loss. There are good risks and foolish risks. As a school we certainly encourage the risks to gain. We want students to try things: a new sport, a new class, a more challenging class, or an artistic performance. Not getting the part in the play is not so important as trying for the part. There is nothing to lose. The risk of cheating on the test may very well be a higher grade; but even the potential short term gain from such a risk may result in a long-term loss. Maybe cheating will become a habit, not uncovered until the loss is devastating; maybe it will get discovered and then have the negative of a loss of integrity, which covers more than just one class. There is the physical risk-taking behavior, skiing as fast as possible to win the race or drinking vodka faster than others to win—prestige?

Certainly all decisions are not political. Some are clearly moral and ethical. But as soon as those latter decisions affect another person they move into the realm of politics. If the opportunity to steal presents itself and the individual does not steal, the decision is personal and moral. No other person may know of that decision. Good will could be the Kantian universal, and if the vast majority of the society adopted that moral precept it would become a political precept.

"Kant does not deny the existence of evil; rather, he emphasizes that precisely because the world of politics is so messy, moral philosophy cannot depend on what happens in it, otherwise men would have no ideals. And without ideals there would be no basis for the human rights outlined, for example, in the Declaration of Independence: rights that are indisputable because, like the Founders, we wish them without contradiction to be universal.

Kant symbolizes a morality of intentions rather than consequences, a morality of abstract justice rather than of actual result. He cares about goodness or badness of a rule, while politics is about the goodness of a specific act in a specific circumstance, since the same rule might produce good results in one situation and bad results in another. Kant's subject is pure integrity, while politics deals with justification, for if an act is justifiable by its likely results, no matter how sordid some of the inner motivations behind it, some measure of integrity is still inherent in the decision-making process." (Kaplan, 112-113)

I feel like I am standing in the engine between the rails of the train tracks looking over the plains into the distance. One rail is politics, one is morality; in the distance they seem to merge. The philosopher would like them to merge; the train driver would not.

AND SO

I may or may not have the toughest job in the school, somewhat like an engineer that tries to teach history and western philosophy while driving the train. I have more influence over the pace than the direction, but from time to time there are junctions where choices have to be made. An important point for me is that I enjoy my job and have enough confidence that I am more than marginally competent. A second important point is that my job is important; it has very little "busy work". While I do not always know what makes teenagers tick, the more I do know the better I am able to work successfully with them, preparing them for the new challenges of adulthood. That same commitment to knowing more in order to benefit students applies to the school as a whole.

I certainly have doubts and regrets, but if I did not I would be myopic. I know I keep learning, and overconfidence is not one of my weaknesses, at least never for very long. What sometimes is viewed as waffling (on the one hand, but on the other), is I hope more appropriately an attempt at balance. Columbine, 9/11 and other major events reflect an imbalance of different people's conflicting goals that existed well before those events. Suicide, alcohol abuse, and hazing exemplify the imbalance on the personal level. Part of my job is to prevent those behaviors, and part is to address them when they happen.

Adults who work with teenagers, and I suspect especially so in residential communities, often relate stories of conversations or letters from former students, team members, dorm residents, or advisees that expressed gratitude for the efforts those adults made on behalf of the teen. Some of those are in the form of apologies from the student for behavior that disappointed the adult.

Sometimes former students simply return unannounced to

reconnect in some fashion. The hockey coach related an incident where a former player returned several years after being dismissed from the school. He was almost unrecognizable, having lost perhaps 100 pounds and appearing quite confident and comfortable. His reconnection was brief, but perhaps he simply wanted to point out to someone who had taken an interest in him that he had grown up.

Another teacher, a dorm parent, relayed that a former student from her dorm had appeared on campus one day with her fiancée looking for both the dorm parent and me. She did not find me, but she had a wonderful conversation with the former dorm parent, who had helped bring about a suspension for alcohol many years earlier.

Adolescence is a period when individuals test themselves and the society around them. Some of these tests result in failures, but the immediate failure—the F on the test, the suspension from school, the expulsion—can itself turn into a longer term success. People learn through tests, but what they learn and how they learn it are crucial as to whether there will be long-term success. The evaluation of the test and its results is as important as the test itself.

I have yet to receive a letter from a former student who was angry at my decision as the Dean. While there may be a variety of reasons for that, I prefer to think that students felt they were treated justly and that they accepted responsibility for their actions. No doubt there are unhappy former students, but they have not put their anger on paper to me.

Putting thoughts on paper is an important teaching tool. It gives the writer a chance to think twice, the second time being the physical act of writing. It also allows for the thoughts to sit and be reviewed as they were written, not as we thought of them. Then they can be edited, or perhaps even tossed. Many of us have written and then regretted sharing those thoughts. On reflection, they seem petty, or hurtful, or downright foolish. The act of writing them is therapeutic, but sometimes those writings are best confined to the flames or the shredder in the 21st century.

Students who had to leave the school often reflect later on the impact that the community or individuals had on them. The ones that matured realize that they had to move on. A return to the place where they failed, in an effort to reverse that failure and to prove to those they had let down that they could succeed, often leads to a second failure. Just as the addict needs to hit bottom before full recovery can begin, so too the student who has been unable to heed the rules of the school needs truly to look in the mirror and be honest with self. Then the letter to the Dean or the dorm parent or the coach has meaning for both the writer and the reader.

I have no doubt that what has happened before is key to what is happening now and that "now" quickly becomes "before." People grow and change, and teenagers do that more than most other ages. I can certainly understand why many adults have no interest in dealing with that age group. For the most part adults want to forget their own transgressions as youth, or if they had few transgressions they do not understand why others have them, and they have little sympathy. But if the adults, the schools, and the society leave the teenagers to their own devices without structure, guidance, assistance, intervention, sympathy and empathy the costs will be much higher for the future. Parenting is hard work; so is educating. They should be partners. Parenting and educating both deserve support by everyone in the society.

Much in life is complex and complicated, and we often look to the simple solution for the complex problem; and we cannot find it. I often think of the Serenity Prayer: Grant me the Serenity to accept what I cannot change, the Courage to change what I can, and the Wisdom to know the difference. We cannot have wisdom if we do not have experience, and teenagers must rely on the adults to get them through the experiences that hopefully will be the foundation for wisdom.

While this book is about me, I cannot resist making it part of the main, a grain of sand in a connected universe. I expect to go back "on duty," and I will face all the same issues and no doubt new ones. And I look forward to it.

WORKS CITED AND OTHER READINGS.

This represents an incomplete list of works that have influenced me, but many of these I read or reread during this past year, particularly during my sabbatical portion of it.

Clinton, Hilary Rodham. *It Takes a Village*. Simon and Schuster: New York, 1996.

Coles, Robert. *The Political Life of Children*. Atlantic Monthly Press: Boston, 1986. *The Moral Life of Children* Atlantic Monthly Press: Boston, 1986.

Crosier, Louis. *Casualties of Privilege*. Avocus Publishing, Inc.: Washington, D.C., 1991.

Goleman, Daniel. *Emotional Intelligence*. Bantam Books: NY 1995.

Hawley, Robert. *The Headmaster's Papers*. 1993.Paul S. Eriksson: Middlebury,VT, 1983.

Herrnstein, Richard J. and Murray, Charles. *The Bell Curve*. The Free Press: New York, 1994.

Johnson, Haynes. *It Was the Best of Times*. Harcourt: New York, 2001.

Kaplan, Robert. *Warrior Politics*, Random House: New York, 2002.

Kindlon, Dan and Thompson, Michael. *Raising Cain: Protecting the Emotional Life of Boys*. Ballantine Books: New York, 1999.

Kozol, Jonathan. *Death at an Early Age*. Houghton Mifflin: Boston, 1967.

Metalious, Grace. *Peyton Place*. Northeastern University Press, Boston, 1999.

Prescott, Peter. *A World of Our Own*. Coward-McCann, Inc.: New York, 1970.

Putnam, Robert. *Bowling Alone*. Simon and Schuster: New York. 2000.

Tatum, Beverly. *Why Are All the Black Kids Sitting Together in the Cafeteria? And Other Conversations About Race*. Basic Books: New York, 1997.

Printed in the United States
6281